Vince Lombardi

Vince Lombardi

His Life and Times

Robert W. Wells

PRAIRIE OAK PRESS
Madison, Wisconsin

Second edition, second printing
First edition, 1971, Wisconsin House, Ltd.
Copyright © 1971 by Robert W. Wells
Copyright renewed 1997
Prairie Oak Press edition copyright © 1997 by Robert W. Wells estate

Prairie Oak Press
821 Prospect Place
Madison, Wisconsin 53703

Printed in the United States of America on acid-free paper
by BookCrafters, Chelsea, Michigan

Library of Congress Cataloging-in-Publication Data

Wells, Robert W.
    [Lombardi]
    Vince Lombardi: his life and times / Robert W. Wells. -- 2nd ed.
       p.   cm. -- (Prairie classics; no. 5)
    Orginally published: Lombardi. 1st ed. Madison, Wis.: Wisconsin House, 1971.
    ISBN 1-879483-43-2
    1. Lombardi, Vince. 2. Football coaches - - United States - - Biography. 3. Green Bay Packers (Football team) - - History.
I. Title. II. Series.
GV939.L6W4 1997
796.332'092 - - dc21   97-40008
[B]   CIP

Foreword to the First Edition

Few sons have the privilege of introducing a book about their father. Fewer have the good fortune to introduce an excellent book about their father. I am one of the privileged and fortunate ones.

My father was a very demanding coach. He demanded of his players dedication, integrity, character and a willingness to pay whatever price necessary in order to attain that highest of human goals—victory. After reading *Vince Lombardi: His Life and Times* I am sure you will agree with me that the author, Robert Wells, could have played for my father.

Vincent H. Lombardi,
St. Paul, Minnesota

Contents

Introduction to the First Edition

I sincerely believe there aren't enough words in the English vocabulary to properly describe Vincent Lombardi. Many stories have been written about Mr. Lombardi—the coach, the person, the humanitarian, the strategist—but somehow after one reviews his fabulous coaching career, as well as his personal life, many of these descriptions fall short. In a relatively short time, Vincent T. Lombardi became a legend. Legends are not born, they are made. And certainly Vincent Lombardi made his. Some people have said he was a great coach. Others have said he was brutal. Still another says he had an inner warmth that forced him to love his players. Whatever the feelings, we all must admit that Vincent Lombardi was one of the most phenomenal men both on and off the field that we've ever known. I knew him personally, both as a football coach and an administrator, and I had personal respect for him in both capacities.

This book then is an account of a legend. It carefully details the labor before the product. We know we are in the presence of a knowledgeable author and a great coach. Lombardi would have liked this book because its vision is not limited: Robert Wells tackles the character of Vincent Lombardi from all sides. The result: Lombardi and the book emerge as blocks of granite.

I am proud to have been associated with the legend of Vincent T. Lombardi.

Elroy L. (Crazylegs) Hirsch
Former Director of Athletics
University of Wisconsin

Chapter 1

"To Win...To Win...To Win..."

In the former French trading post called Green Bay, a midget competing with giants in the football wars, there are few secrets when it comes to the Packers. If a player sneezes in the privacy of the locker room, the fans somehow know about it and are quick to diagnose his case. If a substitute lineman has three poached eggs for breakfast instead of the usual two, the alteration in his routine is a matter for learned comment at Martha's Cafe or Holzer's Drugstore.

But when Vincent T. Lombardi descended on the city like a combination of Captain Bligh, Savonarola, and Emperor Caesar Augustus, not even the wisest curbstone philosophers could have predicted that his coming was the start of an era in professional football unlike any that had gone before.

There was hope when he came, of course. There is always hope before a season starts, and the consensus was that the new man had to do better than the old one. Scooter McLean had been a fine, upstanding coach, no question about that, but he had won only one game and tied one game while losing ten. That was in 1958, the year the Packers had been called a conga team because all they did was go one, two, three, kick. Now in 1959, the portents were improved, but it was not until the final seven minutes of the first regular season game that the happy realization began to emerge among Packer backers that they would have the rare and precious privilege of seeing a football legend take shape.

The date was September 27 and a cold rain was falling. There were 32,150 spectators in City Stadium in Green Bay—a capacity crowd for a change. Tales of Lombardi's training methods and the Packers' four wins of six exhibition games—three more victories than they had managed all last season—had sparked new interest. But the fans were realists—on a per capita basis Green Bay, sometimes called the toilet paper capital of the world because of its principal industry, has more football knowledge than any other city in the land—and a knowledgeable follower of professional sports understands that coaches may come and coaches may go but games are won by the man with the ball. And so, until the game was fifty-three minutes old, not even the most optimistic Green Bay backer imagined that the arrival of a former New York Giants assistant coach to take charge of the faltering franchise would be worth more than a line or two of type in the history of the game.

There had been brave talk, of course, but now the season had started, and the Packers were playing the Chicago Bears and losing. Green Bay's offensive team seemed no better than the one that had cost McLean his job. Only the defensive team offered comfort. It had held the Bears to a forty-six-yard field goal in the first half and another three points early in the fourth quarter. But the way things were going with the offense, Chicago's 6-0 lead seemed big enough.

Some of those huddled in the stands in the rain were catching their first glimpse of Lombardi. Standing near the sidelines in a rumpled tan raincoat, he didn't look very impressive. He had added poundage since his college days, when he had been a 175-pound lineman for Fordham, but he was only five feet nine inches tall, and the players in their helmets and shoulder pads loomed over this stocky fellow with the Brooklyn accent who exulted openly when a play went well and cried out in anger or despair when one failed.

Lamar McHan, the quarterback, gained 101 yards passing. But in Bear territory, it seemed, he either missed his target or the ball bounced out of the receiver's hands. Because the former Chicago Cardinal had been obtained to give the team a leader, Lombardi kept him in the game even after he began to limp from a muscle pull in the second quarter. Bart Starr was on the bench, but in the fall of 1959, even an injured McHan was considered a better bet than Starr, whose future in football was highly doubtful then.

A rugged second-year man from Louisiana State named Jim Taylor was considered a pretty fair ball carrier, the kind of player who enjoyed running into people and trying to knock them down. But the other running back, Paul Hornung, had shown little to inspire enthusiasm since his college days at Notre Dame. There he had been a star, a Golden Boy to the sportswriters and the squealing girls in the stands, but at Green Bay the coaches had never quite known what to do with him. They had been uncertain whether he was a halfback, a fullback, a quarterback, or none of these things, and Hornung had shared their confusion.

The answer came when Lombardi arrived.

"You're my halfback," Vince rasped. "The only way you can get out of the job is to get killed."

Hornung believed him. When Lombardi said a thing, it was so.

Although Hornung and Taylor carried the ball forty-one times between them that afternoon, they did not carry it far enough. Whenever the Packers started to move, a fumble, a penalty, or an incomplete pass returned the ball to the Bears and it was time for the defensive team to grunt and strain and struggle once more.

Now it was the final period. Arms and shoulders ached, leg muscles moved more sluggishly, the bruises hurt, the minds were less alert. It was the time when conditioning tells. The weariness affects everyone, but the man who is in shape is affected less and, whatever its other shortcomings, the Packer team of 1959 was certainly in shape.

The conditioning process its members had survived before the season began was like nothing the players had experienced before. The fine for being overweight was ten dollars a day. The fine for skipping one of the three daily meals was ten dollars. But that was only money. A man could part with money with only a temporary twinge. A worse penalty was the Lombardi tongue.

"Mister," he would yell, tailoring his Brooklyn invective to this bucolic setting, this outpost of America's Dairyland, "you run like a cow."

It was a silly sort of insult. A man might smirk and brush it off if it came from anyone else. But somehow when Lombardi said it, the insult stung.

Even worse than the invective was the necessity to keep going through grass drills and wind sprints when every muscle of the body sent urgent pleas to the weary brain, demanding rest. The grass drills consisted of running hard in one place, flopping onto the belly, leaping up and running again, repeating the process interminably until Vince was finally satisfied. The wind sprints required everyone to run full speed for forty yards or so, then back, doing it again and again until Lombardi said stop.

Phil Bengston, who had come from the San Francisco Forty-Niners to coach the defensive team and would one day attempt the impossible job of filling Lombardi's shoes, told what it was like:

"No one was permitted to dog it. Soon almost all were able to survive. Nobody vomited after the first couple of days."

One member of Bengston's defensive squad, Dave (Hawg) Hanner, lost twenty pounds during the first six weeks of training. The squad lost an average of twelve pounds per man. They groaned and griped when Lombardi was out of earshot, they threatened to quit, to give up football; but finally, they took a reluctant sort of pride in merely being able to survive.

Having learned they could take the worst that this new coach could dish out and still show up for the next day's torture, the men began to believe they could survive anything, including the end of the world. And now it was the fourth quarter of the first game and the Bears had still not been able to approach the Packers' goal.

With eight of the final fifteen minutes gone, Max McGee punted from the Green Bay twenty-nine to the Bears' seventeen. A Chicago rookie fumbled the runback on the twenty-six. Jim Ringo, the Packers' center, threw himself on the ball.

Lombardi was on his feet, pounding his fist against his hand, and McHan went limping out with the rest of the offensive team for what might be the Packers' last chance to score in the new coach's first game.

Whatever those eleven players were thinking then, it seems likely that a single thought crossed several minds: If they came off the field again without a touchdown, the coach would not be pleased.

Although Lombardi had not yet become a living legend, his personality surrounded by an aura of myth and conjecture, he had already managed to arouse mingled feelings of fear, pride, and fierce loyalty in his muscular troops.

He had ended his halftime exhortation by shouting: "Go through that door and bring back victory!" and linebacker Bill Forester had leaped up and cracked his arm against a locker, the most painful injury he was to receive all year. But despite Lombardi's halftime appeal that "Now it's time to score and to win!", they had not scored and time was running out. The order hung over their helmets like a thunderhead as they lined up on the Bears' twenty-six with the clock showing seven minutes left to play.

In those torturous weeks of practice, Lombardi had stressed the basics—blocking and tackling, with the ball carrier looking for a momentary chink in the opponents' living wall and plunging toward it. Now McHan handed off to Hornung. He gained a few difficult yards. The ball went to Taylor, who got his kicks from hitting people, and he picked up a few more. Then it was Hornung's turn and the Bears stopped him, but not until he had made a first down.

On the fifth play after Ringo clutched the fumble, it was up to Taylor. He was five yards away from a score, a long distance on the ground that close to the goal line. The Bears were famous for their defense, but they had not gone through the kind of grass drills and wind sprints that had seemed to be beyond human endurance but somehow were not; they had not survived the degree of organized torture that was to become a Lombardi trademark.

McHan called a play that was to become famous as the Green Bay sweep—an old play, actually, one the Giants had often used while Lombardi was New York's offensive coach. As Taylor followed his blockers around right end and scored, the crowd got a preview of its effectiveness.

Hornung had missed two field goals, one from only fourteen yards out, but he did not miss the extra point and the score was 7 to 6. That was margin enough, although in the last minutes of play while Chicago was desperately trying to put together a final drive, Hawg Hanner tackled the Bears' quarterback, Ed Brown, in the end zone for a safety, making the final score 9 to 6.

When the game ended, Lew Carpenter grabbed Lombardi and the other players converged on them. Inexperienced in staging victory celebrations—they got used to them later—the Packers nearly fumbled their coach in trying to hoist him to their shoulders. But after some cheerful confusion, Vince rode jubilantly toward the dressing room, his teeth bared in a tiger's grin, while the fans yelled and pounded each other on the back and prepared for the biggest unorganized celebration Green Bay had seen in years.

Beating the Bears was always worth a celebration, but this was something more than the happy victory ritual of an afternoon when the smallest city in the league proved it could whip one of the biggest.

Before Lombardi's arrival, the Packers had not only been the worst team in professional ball but the nagging question of whether they belonged in competition with cities ten to a hundred times larger had been raised once more. Now that question had been laid to rest, perhaps for all time.

Lombardi had kept saying he was no miracle man. But he had also said he had not come to lose. As the excitement of his league debut faded, the spectators remembered the fumbles, the missed passes, and the mistakes, but mostly they remembered the final score.

"Winning isn't everything," Lombardi was to say often, when the time came that his words were respectfully recorded as philosophical pearls. "It's the only thing."

The motto doesn't quite make sense under close analysis, but fans understood. The time came when critics protested that such an attitude was unhealthy, that it was a return to a stern, outdated code of conduct, while defenders said yes, it is a return, and about time, too.

The quotation was not yet part of the legend that grew up about this complicated man on the afternoon when the fans jostled their way so happily out of City Stadium. But the fans didn't need to be told that those figures on the scoreboard were what counted, that the lean and hungry days were over, that a new football era had begun in Green Bay.

And not just in Green Bay, for after September 27, 1959, professional football would never again be the same.

Chapter 2

Boyhood in Sheepshead Bay

When the time came that Lombardi was being compared with Knute Rockne by his friends and with Attila the Hun by a few sulky critics, it seemed that he had sprung full blown from obscurity to Green Bay— a leap that some of his eastern buddies might have suggested was not a very long distance. Actually, most of his working life was behind him before he got his chance at a head coaching job in professional football. And behind that working life was a boyhood in Brooklyn that somehow turned out to be exactly the kind of preparation he needed when his big chance came.

Brooklyn is partly a state of mind, a distinctive entity separate from the rest of New York City, with its own dialect and ways of life. Even to most residents of the other four boroughs that make up the unwieldy metropolis, it is unknown turf. Tourists seldom venture off Manhattan Island and few strangers go to Brooklyn except from unavoidable necessity, such as getting lost and failing to get off the subway until too late.

From the west bank of the East River, with the skyscrapers at your back, Brooklyn resembles a great, gray warren filled with undistinguished buildings and inhabited by the kind of people whose outdoor sport is stoopball or kick the can, not football. Actually, of course, Brooklyn is too large and its residents too various for such foolish generalities, now or when young Vincent was growing up.

In his day there, Brooklyn was known mostly for a baseball team whose title came from an outdated nickname—one that was no less a misnomer than that of the Green Bay outfit he would one day coach.

Residents of the Long Island side of the Brooklyn Bridge had been known derisively as "trolley dodgers" at a time when trolleys were the fastest thing to dodge as they hurried across the streets. The title was meant as an insult, and accepted as such at first. But as so often happens, the name stuck after its origin was forgotten, and the ballplayers who performed in the raffish intimacy of Ebbets Field wore it without complaint.

Some of the Brooklyn teams were great and some were terrible, but in general the sentiment they most often aroused was hilarity—the same sort of condescending hilarity that was the traditional reaction of non-Brooklynites to the entire community. When vaudeville was in flower, mention of the borough was a cheap way to get a laugh in a Manhattan theater, although Brooklyn—the Dutch called it Breuckelen—was a flourishing little city when most of the island across the river from it was used only to pasture cows.

Brooklyn was a separate city until 1898, when an uneasy marriage was affected with New York. If the union had not been consummated, it would still be larger than Philadelphia. Its seventy-one square miles are more homogeneous now than they were when Lombardi was young, but it still has good neighborhoods as well as bad ones, along with many that are somewhere between such extremes.

Sheepshead Bay, where Vincent was born to Harry and Matilda Lombardi on June 11, 1913, was an attractive sort of place then, known for its seafood, its fishermen, and the chance it gave recent immigrants to the United States to keep within range of an ocean breeze that reminded them of home.

The sea touched the memories of every Sheepshead Bay native and Lombardi was no exception. It gave him a special view of New York's geography. More than half a century after his birth, he was holding what he called his "Five O'Clock Club" seminar on the balcony of a Florida motel suite. By then his word was considered gospel on almost any subject, including the weather. He studied the sky, noted the wind, and remarked:

"When it's blowing like this from the northeast, it means three days of bad weather."

"Coach," one of the hangers-on said, "you know everything."

The remark was not sarcastic, for Vince's team was about to win its second straight Super Bowl that winter and it was widely assumed that the coach had a pipeline to the angel Gabriel, if not to Gabe's boss.

"When you're brought up on the ocean, you get to know such things," he explained. He was in an affable mood. It was too late to worry about whether the Packers were going to win; he had done all he could for them, and he was relaxed. Still making conversation, he turned to a Manhattan sportswriter.

"You live on the ocean?"

"No," the man answered, not thinking, "I live in New York."

Lombardi flashed the piano keyboard smile that was famous wherever the marvels of televised football had penetrated. The sportswriter felt his stomach muscles tighten.

"Where do you think New York is?" Vince demanded. "It's right on the ocean. Everybody knows New York's right on the ocean."

Later, after he'd had time to brood over the remark while seated at his typewriter, the visitor decided that the exchange had been a significant example of Lombardi arrogance. Actually, it was more symbolic of the schism that forever divides the Brooklynites of Sheepshead Bay from their fellow New Yorkers who live in Manhattan. The canyon dwellers seldom think about Manhattan's being on an ocean, unless they look at a map. They do not think of themselves as seaside folk because if they want to see the open Atlantic it is necessary to go to some place like Jones Beach.

But to a man who was once a boy in Sheepshead Bay, there is no doubt at all that New York is a deep-water port city. The conversation in the Florida motel indicated that Lombardi was still thinking of the world in terms of his special part of Brooklyn even after he'd reached a plateau where he could have had a table at Twenty-One without a reservation.

When Vincent was born, the family lived in a two-story house, which is still there. His aunt lived in it later and his parents remained only a few doors away long after their son had become an important man.

The Lombardis had five children born over a seventeen-year period, so, as the oldest, Vincent was nearly a generation ahead of his youngest brother. Although technically an Italian immigrant, Harry Lombardi arrived in the United States when he was too young to remember much about Italy.

Harry's father had expected to continue his work as a silk merchant when he brought his family to Brooklyn, but it turned out to be a different sort of world. No one wanted to buy his silk, and he went into the hauling business instead. At first, he used horses and wagons, then modernized by buying trucks.

The Lombardis were more prosperous than many of those who had left Europe for a new start in America, but that did not mean that Harry Lombardi could sit around idly. He and his brothers were expected to work in the family business as soon as they were old enough to be of some use. As a young man, Harry automatically went into the trucking business, too, but later became a wholesale butcher. He left home before sunrise to haul meat to Washington Market near the Hudson River, dickered with the buyers from stores and restaurants, made sure he got a fair price by raising his voice and telling them off when they had it coming, then joined them in a friendly chat or a late breakfast after finishing the morning's business.

Harry Lombardi found nothing wrong with the way his father had raised him, and when Vincent was old enough he followed the familiar pattern. The virtues of work were so obvious to families like the Lombardis that they required no discussion. Sons were supposed to help out, as much as they were able, in the old fishing port called Sheepshead Bay. And so Vincent did as the other sons and grandsons of immigrants did in his neighborhood, all of them taking it as a matter of course that a boy's duty was to give up much of his leisure in order to help the family maintain its toehold in the place where immigrants had come seeking opportunities they couldn't find at home.

Looking back, Vince did not consider it an unpleasant boyhood—quite the contrary—and it is likely that it was not. His father's stern sense of duty was tempered by Mrs. Lombardi's warmth. The boy's mother had been one of thirteen children born to a Sheepshead Bay family named Izzo, so Vince and the other children had a plentiful supply of aunts and uncles, nieces, nephews, and cousins, along with a bewildering variety of friends.

It never seemed to matter to Mrs. Lombardi if an extra dozen guests showed up at the last minute for dinner. In those days, no one had detected any signs that Vince could work miracles. But his mother's ability to feed a multitude was regarded as close to supernatural. Hospitality was never rationed.

Vince might bring home Joe Goettischeim, who lived a block away from the house on East Fourteenth Street. When they were old enough, Harold and Joseph, the other two sons, felt free to invite their playmates, and the daughters, Claire and Madeline, brought home friends.

Assorted relatives who were passing by somehow sensed when pasta was boiling. A priest or two might show up. Matilda Lombardi was never sure ten minutes before mealtime whether she'd be serving seven Lombardis or an extra dozen guests. But somehow there was always plenty to go around.

The children accepted this as the normal way of running a household, but when they grew up and had families of their own to feed they remembered and marveled. They also remembered Mrs. Lombardi's ability to understand, her role as the family peacemaker, the one who did not jump to conclusions but thought things out carefully before she acted. Their father's temper was more uncertain. He was a stern disciplinarian whose word was law and who countenanced no back talk.

The contrasting personalities of the parents are a clue to Vince Lombardi's complex personality. He could be dictatorial, driving, demanding, and ambitious, with a mercurial temper and a habit of erupting with anger when a player achieved something too far short of perfection. But he was also a sentimental man, warm and sensitive. He was the sort of fellow who was both hated and loved. If there was much of his father in the man he became, there was an inheritance from his mother, too.

As a boy, Vince worked with his father in the useful but sometimes unpleasant tasks of cutting up beef and pork carcasses, carrying loads of meat, and standing up for his rights in the competitive salesmanship of the wholesale market. To earn respect, he learned early, it is necessary to work hard, do a job right the first time, and not complain.

If a knife slipped in carving a side of beef or a toe was stepped on, it was no big thing. His father had a saying about it.

"Hurt?" he would say. "Hurt is in the mind."

The time came when numerous muscular young men in Green Bay had cause to wish Harry Lombardi had chosen some less Spartan form of wisdom to instill in his oldest son. The first lesson in this branch of the Lombardi philosophy was presented for their consideration on the new coach's second day in town. He found a dozen of his players awaiting treatment in the trainer's room.

"What's this?" he roared. "You've got to play with those small hurts."

Any player able to walk left at once. At times the coach felt that his men would learn something only if he pounded it into their thick skulls, day after day after day, but the Packers picked up this lesson quickly. From that moment on, it was understood that anything less than a broken leg was no excuse for staying off the football field. The voice in the training room was Vince's, but the theory that lent it power was imported all the way from Sheepshead Bay.

"He tolerates perfection," it was said of Lombardi in the days when he was the ruling monarch of professional football, "providing it is real good."

His players were not the only ones who felt this. After a reception in his honor in Washington, where he had gone to coach the Redskins, Rene Carpenter, former wife of astronaut Scott Carpenter, told how his entrance had affected her.

"All of a sudden my skirt was too short and my back was too bare," she said. "We were reduced to feeling like children."

It is highly unlikely that Lombardi would have criticized her costume—unless, of course, she had arrived in a football uniform and had the helmet on wrong. His friends usually found him affable enough away from the football field, although one who had known him intimately for years said his reaction was much like that of Mrs. Carpenter's.

"You were afraid to do something wrong in front of him" the friend said, expressing a feeling common among those who dealt with this man who made a career of insisting that any effort less than 100 percent— some said 110 percent—was not good enough.

The same sort of thing might have been said about Harry Lombardi, the meat wholesaler, although his influence was confined to his family for the most part. According to those who knew the elder Lombardi as children, the coach's insistence that there were two ways to do a thing, the wrong way and the Lombardi way, also owed a debt to parental example.

In his later years, when Vince had his reputation made, the legend grew up that he had worked hard and long as a youth because he was so poor. In truth, the Lombardis were a long way from poverty. They had a pleasant house in a decent neighborhood and enough money for all the necessities and some of the minor luxuries. If they worked hard, that was merely how things were done in that time and place.

Whatever the cause of the driving ambition that was analyzed so often when Vince Lombardi became a celebrity, it was not an unhappy childhood. Along with the work, there was fun. "Anything could turn into a party," says a man who remembered life at the Lombardi house in Sheepshead Bay.

It is hard to know now whether there was rebellion against the strict discipline. If so, it was short lived. When he was grown, Lombardi regarded his father with deep affection.

"He was a perfectionist," he once said, and he meant the description as a compliment. "He was a perfectionist if there ever was one."

For example, at one time the elder Lombardi decided to fix up the basement under the gray frame house and to tear down an old barn out back that had once housed horses. Vince helped, of course. He was old enough to have ideas of his own about how the job should be done.

But the way it was done was Harry Lombardi's way, with ready criticism for imperfections and equally quick praise for a job done right. When the new concrete floor in the basement had hardened and the task had passed inspection, the boy was paid in hard cash. There were no allowances in the Lombardi family. Money was to be earned.

The fixed lines of authority in families like Vincent's were so well understood that questioning them was pointless. There was room, however, for a boy to have his own enthusiasms, and, like most healthy young males, Vince developed an absorbing interest in sports while still in grammar school. With baseball the big league sport around Brooklyn, he followed the misfortunes of the Dodgers each summer, but even then football was more interesting to him.

His friend Joe Goettischeim—they were altar boys at St. Mark's Catholic Church nearby—was only mildly interested in football and preferred the movies. Vince had nothing against movies either, but when the Giants were in town during the football season Joe somehow found himself going to the Polo Grounds instead of the theater. Mild mannered most of the time, now that he was twelve, with strangers Vince gave the impression of being shy. But if you were his friend, Joe discovered, you usually did what he wanted to do.

The Polo Grounds was not handy to Sheepshead Bay. Joe sometimes put up an argument when Vince proposed the long subway ride, as on an afternoon when he told Joe they had to go because he wanted to see Bo Molenda play. Not many Sheepshead Bay boys had heard of Bo Molenda, but Vince knew all about him. Thus the two boys rode from the far reaches of Brooklyn to the Polo Grounds because that was what Vince wanted to do.

Chapter 3

Fordham's Testing Ground

At one point in his boyhood, Lombardi planned to become a priest. It was a natural enough ambition for the oldest son of a devout Catholic family, particularly one where friendly members of the cloth were apt to drop in frequently to sample Mrs. Lombardi's cooking.

Some years later, when Vince was coaching the Packers and known widely for his refusal to consider second place worth having, friends speculated about what might have happened if he'd gone into the priesthood. While it would have been a loss to football, they said, it would have been quite an honor for Sheepshead Bay to be known as the birthplace of the first American pope.

Even as an altar boy at St. Mark's, Vince exercised his competitive spirit. A friend and rival, Paul Morris, sometimes complained that in the procession he always had to be a candlebearer while Vince always got to carry the cross. The altar boy with the cross went first, so that was the place of honor. Perhaps young Lombardi wanted the honor more than Paul. Looking back on those days years later, Morris remembered that one thing about Vincent—he always got to carry the cross.

At Public School 206, Lombardi was no troublemaker—he was too self-disciplined for that. But the other boys recognized his fiery temper. Hearts, a card game in which the queen of spades counts thirteen points against the holder, was a favorite pastime after school, and it was considered great fun to stick Vince with the black queen because it made him so furious.

Still thinking of becoming a priest, Lombardi went to Cathedral High School and then transferred to St. Francis Preparatory School. It was there that he decided his future was in sports. His coach was Harry Kane, a man the boys looked upon with considerable respect because he had once been closely associated with greatness.

When Kane was at another New York school, Commerce High, he had coached a left-handed first baseman who went on to the New York Yankees and batted cleanup behind Babe Ruth. Helping to develop the remarkable athletic skills of a Lou Gehrig might seem like glory enough to last a high school coach a lifetime, but Kane will also go down in sports history as the fellow who taught Vince Lombardi football.

Vince also played baseball at St. Francis but, as far as is known, Kane never compared his prowess with a bat with Gehrig's. He became something of a star on the football field, however, although he did it more on determination than anything else. At less than 175 pounds, he was not the overpowering kind of fullback, but when he had the ball he was a battler who was tough to bring down. In his senior year, he rated an invitation to Fordham from "Sleepy Jim" Crowley.

In the early thirties, it was comparatively simple for some schools to build a football team. It was said—with some exaggeration, no doubt—that coaches simply drove a bus into the Pennsylvania coal mining towns and filled it with muscular young men who were scholarly enough to sign an X on the dotted line. If a player could tear a book in two, it didn't matter whether he knew how to read it.

Having to contend with the Jesuits who ran Fordham University, however, Crowley was somewhat handicapped in his recruiting. Some of the good fathers considered football a waste of time. Although others were among the most enthusiastic rooters, the rule laid down was that a football player had to be able to learn something besides how to block and tackle. Before he handed out one of the twenty-two athletic scholarships allotted to football each year, Crowley checked a lad's scholastic record almost as carefully as his gridiron ability.

Lombardi had good grades, and he was delighted to be offered the scholarship. Next to Notre Dame, Fordham was the leading football power among the Catholic colleges—under Crowley, its teams won 56, lost 13, tied 7, the best percentage attained by any coach in that school's history. Furthermore, Vince knew Crowley had been a member of the Notre Dame backfield that Grantland Rice had called the Four Horsemen of the Apocalypse. Having someone so celebrated take an interest in him was enough to make Vince say yes to the offer without a second thought.

Crowley wanted to be sure he understood the arrangement. As long as he kept his grades up, the coach told the boy, he would get his room, board, tuition, and the price of his books. In return, he was expected to play football.

"What if I get hurt?"

"If you're injured or if you don't make the team, you keep the scholarship. But then you'll have to do some other kind of work around the campus."

It seemed a businesslike arrangement, and Lombardi accepted. He had no intention of not making the team but when he showed up for the first practice session it was quickly apparent that Fordham didn't really need a 175-pound fullback. What it needed was another lineman, but Vince seemed too small for that job on a team that relied mainly on its defensive abilities to win games.

Frank Leahy, who would later be head coach at Notre Dame, was Crowley's assistant. He motioned to Lombardi, told him to line up, then threw a block that sent him sprawling. Vince picked himself up and suggested they try that again. This time, Leahy was the one who was knocked down and that was how Lombardi became a Fordham guard.

He was assigned number forty and placed in the line next to Alex Wojciechowicz, one of the biggest men on the team and among the most talented. If Alex had doubts about playing shoulder to shoulder with a 175-pounder, he soon lost them.

"He doesn't take any guff from anybody," Wojciechowicz said of Lombardi, neatly summarizing character without wasting words.

When Lombardi had qualified as an authority on the national scene by coaching a team that won for Green Bay, his discussions of the advantages of discipline became familiar to the public as well as to the players who were well paid to listen to them. It is plain that his attitude toward the establishment of a firm line of authority was a logical result of his youthful training.

Like so many of the other men who influenced Vince in his malleable years, Sleepy Jim Crowley was a stern disciplinarian—Leahy was no soft touch, either. Their way of running a football squad followed a Fordham custom established by Crowley's predecessor, Frank Cavanaugh.

Called "the Iron Major," Cavanaugh operated as if Fordham was a Marine boot camp. His players were mostly young men a generation or two away from Ireland, Italy, Poland, or Lithuania who had been used to doing what the old man said at home and didn't go off in a corner and sulk if someone in authority yelled at them.

The Iron Major had been an artillery officer in World War I. The Germans had managed to hit him in the head with portions of a high explosive shell, but it had slowed him down only temporarily. As Fordham coach from 1927 through 1932, he had established a tradition that Crowley and Leahy upheld—rigid discipline, tough conditioning, a hard-nosed attitude toward playing with injuries.

Fordham had only sixteen hundred students when Lombardi enrolled there, but its teams played such big schools as New York University. The Rams represented more than the college. They understood without being told that they were carrying the hopes of hundreds of thousands of New Yorkers who had never seen the campus in the Bronx—immigrants or sons and daughters of immigrants, Roman Catholics generally, the great body of fans who had a little trouble identifying with an Ivy League school like Columbia.

College football had got its start in the East, but by the early 1930s the balance of power had moved away from that region and was centered in the Midwest, with strong enclaves in the South and Far West. The wind of de-emphasis was already blowing across some eastern campuses. There was even talk of it at Fordham, although it was not yet much of a threat to Sleepy Jim Crowley and his Rams. Eastern football fans, some of whom could remember a time when a Michigan-Yale game was considered a mismatch because the New Haven boys were so much better, were not happy with their new role of intersectional underdogs. When those tough Polish, Irish, and Italian kids who played for the Rams smote the upstarts from Purdue or Pitt or Georgia, it was heartening proof that the East wasn't dead yet.

An admirer of Sigmund Freud might see some significance in the fact that a region which was on the defensive, when it came to football, identified with a team which made such a specialty of defense. In 1929, while Lombardi was still a high school boy and the Iron Major was in charge at Fordham, the Rams' line was so hard to move that an anonymous Associated Press caption writer called it the Seven Blocks of Granite. The name caught on. It was retained through the 1930 season, then regretfully allowed to die as the resident Blocks graduated and no equally immovable lads stepped forward to take their places.

It was too good a gimmick to be abandoned forever, and Tim Cohane revived it for the line that included Lombardi. Cohane was charged with the Rams' public relations and, as a clever young Irishman who went on to become a nationally celebrated sportswriter, he could see no reason why the phrase could not be used again, particularly as the teams of 1934 through 1937 were at least as hard to shove around as the ones of 1929 and 1930.

It was the school's boast that no one could score a touchdown through the Fordham line, although sometimes an opponent quit trying the impossible and chose to run around the Granite Blocks or throw a pass over their stubborn heads.

After the required apprenticeship on the freshman team, Lombardi joined the line as a sophomore guard in the fall of 1934. His future did not seem secure, however. That year's frosh squad included a rugged young guard named Ed Franco, who was destined to become an All-American. According to campus rumor, as soon as Franco became a sophomore Lombardi would have to go sit on the bench.

The talk reached Marie Planitz, the sister of a Fordham student and the future Mrs. Lombardi. She and Vince met Franco in an ice cream parlor near the campus one evening. Marie looked him over very carefully.

"So you're Ed Franco," she said. "You're the fellow who's going to take my boyfriend's job."

Certain he couldn't do it, she bet Ed a box of candy that he couldn't. It would have been an interesting confrontation—the Franco talent against the Lombardi determination—but it never took place and no one won the bet. When Franco became a sophomore, Crowley decided he needed both him and Lombardi in the lineup and he made Franco into a tackle instead of a guard.

From 1935 through 1937, Crowley had perhaps the best defensive team in the land. It shut out its opponents thirteen times during those three seasons, including three scoreless ties with another hard-nosed outfit, Jock Sutherland's Pitt Panthers.

It was Crowley's theory that one way to create the kind of team spirit that produced shutouts of tough opponents was to encourage an almost mystical feeling of esprit de corps. To win, it was necessary to want to win so deeply that it became a temporary obsession that ended only when the game was over. Then it was necessary to start building up the same unreasoning feeling about next Saturday's opponents.

At many schools, where a football game was only a game, a willingness to do and come as close as necessary to dying for alma mater was already considered a quaint throwback to more naive times. But not among Sleepy Jim's Rams. Their attitude was typified by a custom the guards and tackles had of staring straight into the opponents' eyes during that long moment of tension after the opening kickoff when the linemen crouched, ready to spring into action when the ball was snapped for the game's first play.

There was no talk. There was just the open-eyed and menacing stare before the two lines crashed together, the opponents flesh and sinew meeting the Rams' granite barrier. The Fordham stare was a psychological weapon that the players were convinced gave them an edge.

No inquiring scientist ever crept between the lines to record whether Vincent Lombardi's stare was more menacing than that of Alex Wojciechowicz or Johnny Druze or Al Babartsky. But that moment of terrifying silence as the college boys made ready to fight for Fordham was fine training for Vince's future as the most successful professional coach in history. The time came when it was widely believed that the look he gave a Packer who had failed to achieve perfection was able to curdle human blood at a hundred paces.

The Rams had another custom that played a role in Lombardi's days as Green Bay's resident genius. Even during a time when some of the young men employed by the Packers were national celebrities, they were expected to stand up and sing to a critical audience of their fellow players. It was part of the initiation of rookies to arise and make fools of themselves before the veterans by stumbling through a song, but the old-timers were not exempt from such childish games.

Song was a part of football, Lombardi believed, and the notion can be traced back to those bus rides he took with the Rams to the Polo Grounds where Fordham played its home games in the middle 1930s.

Joseph Maniaci was elected captain of the Rams in 1935 when Vince was a junior, and another backfield man, Frederick Maulte, got the honor in 1936. Andy Palau, the quarterback, got the glory of winning the school's Madow Trophy. When the game was over, the headlines usually went to someone besides Lombardi—even Big Alex got his share, although no copyreader contends with a name like Wojciechowicz if he can avoid it.

But there was one place where Harry Lombardi's boy was the acknowledged leader. Riding from the Rose Hill campus to the Polo Grounds on the school bus, the guard from Sheepshead Bay led the singing. Vince didn't have the most melodious voice perhaps, but it was loud and it had spirit. When he came to the line in one of the school songs that pledged "we'll do or die," no listener could doubt that young Lombardi was planning to do exactly what the song said when those dastards from Pitt or NYU or Southern Methodist dared challenge Fordham's Seven Blocks of Granite.

Chapter 4

Disciplining a Block of Granite

Father Harold Mulqueen, a gruff but friendly Irishman, stayed at Fordham so long that he lived from a time when he was considered too easygoing to a time when he was considered far too strict with the young. He was in charge of St. John's Hall when it was the home of Vince Lombardi.

St. John's held about half of the two hundred fifty students who lived and boarded on the campus in those days—the other fourteen hundred commuted from their homes in the New York area. The football players were assigned to St. John's, so it was more prestigious than its rival dormitory.

Father Mulqueen was charged with enforcing rules of conduct that the students of today would consider medieval. Even in the 1930s, males who attended many colleges could come and go as they pleased, although the coeds were subject to regulations designed to encourage virginity or, at least, discreetness. But the Jesuits who ruled Fordham had no coeds to worry about, and they intended to put up with very little folderol from the boys in their charge.

St. John's had a compulsory study period from 7:30 to 10 P.M., Sunday through Thursday. On Friday night, as a concession to the college boys' animal spirits, they could stay out until 10 P.M. The bars were lowered even further on Saturdays, when curfew did not sound until an hour before midnight. If a night owl wanted to wander around past 11 P.M. he could seek special permission from the school authorities, but his story had better be foolproof or he wouldn't get it.

Mondays through Fridays, attendance at 7:30 A.M. mass was compulsory. Saturday was a free day—even attendance at the football game was voluntary except for the players—but on Sunday every resident student was expected to go to mass at 8 A.M., even if he'd stayed out until 11 P.M. the night before.

Father Mulqueen, as the fellow in charge of enforcing of the rules, did not expect any back talk. He was as enthusiastic a follower of football as there was on the campus—and in those days, that was saying quite a bit—but that didn't mean he intended to let any of the resident players get away with a thing. That included the Seven Blocks of Granite.

The priest had his own notions about discipline, however. If a boy was caught sneaking in past curfew or violating one of the other numerous rules of behavior, he was supposed to be sent to the college's central office. That meant a letter home and possibly suspension from classes. Suspension would be bad enough—these were mostly kids from poor families who knew their only chance to rise out of the hand-to-mouth existence they'd known was to get a college degree. But the letter home was even more feared. Lombardi knew what would happen if Harry Lombardi got such a message, and most of the other boys would have also been in serious trouble if their fathers were told that they were goofing off instead of taking advantage of this chance to rise into the exclusive ranks of the college educated.

Thus, when one of his charges committed an infraction of the rules, Mulqueen gave him a choice. He could be sent to the central office, leading to heaven knows what complications, or he could take his chances with the good father, the punishment to be inflicted at once.

Almost invariably, the boy preferred Mulqueen's justice to the hullabaloo that a trip to the central office would arouse. When caught, he would bend over and the priest would swat him. In most cases, Mulqueen used a broken drumstick that he had appropriated from the band's supplies when it was of no further use to the musicians—the drumstick was still among the priest's cherished souvenirs thirty-five years later. If the infraction was more serious, the cigar-smoking Irishman used a length of light cord into which he had tied a number of knots. Mulqueen was a tall and vigorous man, the knotted wire whistled through the air with enthusiasm, and a young man would think twice before trying to get away with something again.

Lombardi did not need to be lashed with a light cord to understand that rules are to be obeyed. But he was also a youth who responded to a challenge, and trying to outwit Mulqueen was a game where the stakes were high enough to be worthwhile. For example, one evening in 1936 after seeing his boys safely in their beds shortly after the study period ended at 10, the priest walked over to the Jesuit residence on the campus to chat with friends.

About 11 P.M., he headed back toward St. John's Hall. As was his habit—he understood boys—he moved very quietly when he neared the dormitory. He opened the front door without making a sound. All was quiet. He started toward the stairway that led to the sleeping quarters.

He stopped short. Creeping down the stairs, shoes in hand, were two members of the Fordham Rams. One was a substitute, a large young man named Jim Lawlor. Keeping pace with him, treading very carefully in his stocking feet, was the future head coach and general manager of the Green Bay Packers.

The priest reached for his drumstick and headed for the stairs. The boys stood frozen for a moment. Then, without a word, they pivoted on the stairs and headed back toward their room, still holding their shoes, still tiptoeing.

Mulqueen was a dedicated disciplinarian but he was also Irish and his ancestry played him false. He should have leaped up the stairs, ready to beat a mighty tattoo on those tempting targets, but he couldn't do it. The sight of those two muscular young men mincing along, pretending they hadn't intended to sneak out and get into some devilment, struck him as hilarious.

He had to laugh. He didn't want to laugh—it was bad for discipline—but he couldn't help himself. By the time he'd enjoyed the best laugh he'd had in weeks he was no longer in the mood to swat anybody and he went chuckling off to bed. For several days, Lawlor and Lombardi lived in fear of what might happen, but Mulqueen never had the heart to punish the pair that had given him such an enjoyable moment.

Lombardi was not always so lucky, however. He roomed with Lawlor, a lad who was willing to take chances, and one night Mulqueen strode into the room and accused Jim of having been out after curfew. Jim admitted his guilt and received several hearty whacks from the trusty drumstick that the priest pulled out from under his cassock.

Lombardi sat on the other bed, laughing at how his friend was suffering. The priest turned on him.

"If he went out, you must have been out, too," he told Vince and began swatting him with the drumstick. If Lombardi wasn't guilty that time, he had it coming for some nights the prefect didn't know about, so he held no grudge.

Usually he stayed out of trouble, but he was not one to remain a spectator when a contest was in progress, and the sport at St. John's Hall involved trying to outwit Harold Mulqueen. The priest's favorite technique in trying to stop the crap games held in the dorm was to stroll about, seemingly immersed in reading his breviary like the holy man he was, but listening constantly for the click of dice or the muffled cries of "eight's the point" or "come on seven."

If a telltale sound was heard, the prefect went bounding into the room, laying about him with his knotted light cord until the players fled, then confiscating the loot for the mission fund. Over the years, he raised a considerable sum to minister to the heathens by this method, but none of it came from the crap games run by the partnership of Lawlor and Lombardi.

They did not play in the early stages but acted as the bank, in return for providing the room and outwitting Father Mulqueen. They collected a nickel a pass until they'd built up a ten dollar stake, then risked it. If they lost the ten, they'd go back to cutting the game again, a system that ensured that any money lost was not their own.

Lombardi's role was to make sure that if the priest was within listening distance the game was played in utter silence. Crap games and disciplined quiet do not go together, so it is proof of Vince's ability to enforce rules even as a college boy that Father Mulqueen never caught on.

Such fun and games loom large in the memories of Lombardi's generation of Fordham students. Actually, however, college for Vince and most of the other young men was mostly a matter of hard work to meet the high standards set for them. For the football players, it was also a time when it was necessary to keep up the scholastic standards while spending most of their spare time working for Sleepy Jim Crowley and his assistants.

When Lombardi was a senior, it seemed certain that all the bruises and hard work were going to pay off. The 1936 team was a favorite to go to the Rose Bowl, which was not then monopolized by the Big Ten and Pacific Eight champions. Fordham had never played in a bowl game and harbored a deep suspicion that Notre Dame hogged the honors among Catholic colleges.

But 1936 seemed to be different. "Rose Hill to Rose Bowl" banners went up on the campus in the Bronx soon after the season started, and the Rams rose to the challenge. They won the first four games, including a victory over those worthy representatives of the Protestant Southwest, Southern Methodist. Pittsburgh was next, the team that had held the Rams scoreless and been held scoreless in return in 1935. This time, Crowley suggested, it might be nice if the team scored some points. In the Pitt dressing room Jock Sutherland made a similar suggestion. But when the game was over, the scoreboard read 0-0 once again.

Pitt was one of the country's top teams and a tie was no disgrace. Next the Rams beat Purdue 15 to 0, giving eastern sports writers a chance to point out that the Big Ten was only cow country after all. Then came Georgia and a 7-7 tie.

The Rams were still unbeaten. On the opposite coast, the mills of the football gods ground out the informal word that Fordham could have a Rose Bowl invitation if it would accept it. But one game remained and at Rose Hill in the Bronx it was decided to wait.

New York University was Fordham's traditional rival. In 1935, the Rams had whipped NYU 21 to 0. It was generally conceded that the 1936 Fordham team was even better, and NYU's squad was, if anything, worse than a year ago. So there was no hurry about the Rose Bowl. It seemed better to delay until the season was over, the formality of victory over NYU out of the way. Then the invitation could be accepted and the rejoicing begun.

The Depression was not as deep as in 1932 or 1933, but many New Yorkers still had time on their hands and plenty of leisure to sit around and discuss the finale to the season. The interest built up to the point where it was decided that the Polo Grounds was not big enough. The game was moved to Yankee Stadium so more tickets could be sold. When Saturday arrived, more than 82,000 spectators showed up, the largest crowd to see Fordham play before or since.

Riding the bus to the stadium, with Lombardi leading the songs, the team was full of confidence—or, perhaps, overconfidence. The talk was not as much of NYU as of the Rose Bowl. For Vince and the other seniors, the trip to the West Coast would be a glorious climax to their college playing days.

Around Rose Hill, when you talk with football men who remember that day in 1936, you can still hear attempts to explain what happened.

To a man, they agree the Rams had a better team. But it was one of those games where nothing went the way it was supposed to go.

NYU's team had very little at stake—no matter what happened, it would go to no bowl game. It played with the abandon that is associated with the underdog. Its punter kept booting the ball so that Fordham had to start its drive on the two- or three-yard line. The Rams would push and shove and struggle, making progress toward the enemy goal. But then they would lose momentum. Even worse, they would lose the ball. Before long, the punter was booming one back to the coffin corner and they had to do the same job all over again.

The best Fordham could do was a pair of field goals. If the Seven Blocks of Granite could do as well as they had against Pitt, SMU, and Purdue, the six points would be plenty. But they were not able to keep the NYU team scoreless. It was of some slight satisfaction that the touchdown wasn't scored through the line, the runner skirting around the end of the granite wall. But the final score was 7 to 6.

And so Fordham did not go to the Rose Bowl. The folks at Pasadena no longer wanted the Rams. The Orange Bowl promoters were less particular, but it would have been humiliating to settle for second best and Fordham turned them down.

No one who played on the 1936 Fordham team ever quite forgot that loss to NYU or the things that were said about it—even so friendly a critic as Tim Cohane explained that the Rams had come down with an epidemic of "headline catarrh." It was an important part of Vince Lombardi's education.

It demonstrated once again that a team that's up can whip a better team that's taking things for granted. It reinforced the lesson that the world has few rewards for good losers. It became a basic example in his development of a philosophy about football in the days when he was both a coach and a self-appointed team psychologist.

Second was nowhere. When you came in second, you got invited to the Orange Bowl, not the Rose Bowl. You went from being a hero to a bum. You had to listen to people tell you why you lost instead of having them come around, hat in hand, to inquire respectfully how you'd won.

Lombardi played that game over and over again in his mind. Later, when he was riding high, he sometimes told friends that he regretted not having been head coach at Fordham. He was not talking about the college that abandoned varsity football from 1943 to 1946 and from 1955 to 1963, however, or the Fordham of recent years, its days as a major gridiron power behind it. He meant the Fordham of the days when Sleepy Jim Crowley was in charge and the line was as hard to budge as a granite wall.

If it had worked out that Lombardi had taken over a team like that, things would have been different. The tackling would have been crisp, the blocking certain. And when the Rams were leading 6 to 0 and an NYU back headed around the end of the line, someone would have tackled him for a loss, and 82,000 spectators in Yankee Stadium would have leaped to their feet and cheered.

Somehow, Lombardi and the other members of the 1936 team survived the NYU upset. It seems likely that Vince took it harder than most, however. He hated to lose at anything, then or later. He hated to lose at golf, when the time came that he played the game. He hated to lose at bridge or gin rummy. Especially he hated to lose at football, and he often blamed himself when a team he was associated with came in second.

At Fordham, he hated to lose in the scholastic competition, too, especially to a friend. Wellington Mara, who later became his boss on the New York Giants, ranked third in the class and Leo Paquin, Vince's fellow lineman, ranked fifth.

"I'll get you guys," he'd say when the list of grades came out, but they stayed ahead.

When he graduated, he ranked seventh. That was good enough so he had a cum laude ranking, but Paquin and Mara were still ahead of him.

In 1937, the Fordham team got revenge by beating NYU handily. In fact, its string of victories was interrupted only by the customary scoreless tie with Jock Sutherland's Panthers. The Rams ranked third that year, but Lombardi was no longer there and so the 1937 season could not make up for what had happened in the last game of 1936.

There were more pleasant memories to take with him into the difficult outside world of 1937. He might not have been the star of the team, but he could always say he'd been a part of the line that the sportswriters called the Seven Blocks of Granite. He could point out to prospective employers that he'd spent a consistent four years on the dean's list, despite all the time spent on the football field. He could also take satisfaction from the knowledge that he'd lived up to his father's teaching that "hurt is in the mind."

When he told his players some years later that a man must learn to live with pain, he could cite the example of the 1936 game between Fordham and Pittsburgh, the second of their three successive scoreless ties. The game was about half over and the Panthers had the ball on Fordham's two-yard line. The lines came together. Big Alex Wojciechowicz stopped the runner, but in the melee Al Barbatsky, who played on the other side of Lombardi, was knocked groggy and Vince took an elbow in the mouth.

Vince was bleeding and Al could hardly stand, but neither was willing to come out. Pitt was stopped. The game continued with the two injured players still in the lineup—in those days of one-platoon football, a man was expected to play sixty minutes. When the game was over, Lombardi lay on the table while Dr. Gerry Carroll took thirty stitches to close his wound.

"When I got home that night," Vince liked to say in telling this story with a moral, "I certainly was hurting in my mind."

Graduation day came on June 16, 1937. Of the three hundred young men who stepped forward to accept their diplomas, all but one wore black shoes with their caps and gowns. The exception was the twenty-four-year-old Lombardi.

The time came when the coach they called St. Vincent was a favorite subject of cocktail party psychoanalysts and it might have been said in such discussions that his refusal to conform at the solemn graduation ceremony was a sign of rebellion against the Establishment—or, perhaps, a way to grab the spotlight. But when a friend asked Lombardi why he had set his own style in graduation day footwear, he had a simpler explanation.

"I like white shoes," he said, and perhaps that was reason enough.

Chapter 5

St. Cecelia's $22 Bargain

Because of a late start in college, caused mostly by his youthful hesitancy over whether to enter the priesthood, Lombardi was two or three years behind most young men his age and he wanted to make up for lost time. But jobs were scarce in 1937—so scarce that he finally decided to go back to Fordham and qualify for a law degree. Meanwhile, he picked up spending money by playing part time for a minor league football team, the Brooklyn Eagles, and by working as an insurance adjustor, a job for which it seems likely he had some natural talent.

In the summer of 1939, he was earning twenty dollars a week at du Pont in Wilmington, Delaware, when another former member of the Seven Blocks of Granite, Leo Paquin, suggested a job he'd like better. Andy Palau, coach at St. Cecelia's High School in Englewood, New Jersey, and team quarterback while they were in college, needed an assistant.

Lombardi went to New Jersey to see about it. The job was a step up financially—it paid twenty-two dollars a week—and it would give Vince a chance to get back into sports. His acceptance meant dropping out of law school, which he'd been attending partly on his father's advice.

For its money, the parochial school got a bargain. Lombardi not only worked as Palau's assistant during football season but he also coached basketball and baseball and handled a full schedule as a classroom teacher of chemistry, physics, and Latin.

The following summer, he picked up some extra money assisting the director of a summer sports camp and, as a sideline, worked as the paid umpire of high school baseball games. In 1940, he felt secure enough financially to marry Marie Planitz of Red Bank, New Jersey, the one he'd been dating during most of his years at Fordham.

They found an apartment in the vicinity and Lombardi settled down to the life of a small school faculty member. He was not getting much money, but that didn't mean he took the job lightly. Marie learned early in their marriage that her husband took games at St. Cecelia's as seriously as he would later those involving crews of highly paid athletes.

Palau still had the main responsibility for the high school football team but Vince was given a free hand with the basketball squad. He knew very little about it, but he went about learning. Night after night, he stayed up until 2 A.M. picking the brains of other coaches. Before long, he was showing them some tricks they hadn't taught him.

Around Englewood they still talk about a game played during his second year at St. Cecelia's. The other team was from Bogota, New Jersey, one of the highest scoring outfits in the state. Lombardi brooded about the matter for a while. Then he gathered his players around him and issued his orders.

The parochial school boys had already discovered that the way to get along with Coach Lombardi was to do exactly as he said. He had told them that they could beat Bogota if they kept the ball away from the other team, and that's what they did.

The rules were different in those days. High school teams were happy to settle for thirty points or so a night. Still, the final score of the game with Bogota was startling enough to get Lombardi's name on the national sports wires for the first time since he'd left Fordham. St. Cecelia's won, 6 to 1.

The stalling tactics that held the rival school to a single free throw made the Bogota coach furious, but that was not important. The important thing was that Vince's team had won.

Winning got to be a habit. During his eight years as a high school basketball coach, his teams won 105 and lost only 57 even though St. Cecelia's was a comparatively small school that had often been considered an easy mark by some of its larger rivals. One year, it won the state championship—the first in its history.

Parochial school sports were taken seriously. Grammar school talent was scouted and steps were taken to try to persuade a likely lad to choose one school instead of another for his high school career. Lombardi had

friends, inside the church and out, and he held his own with his rival high
school coaches in the backstage wheeling and dealing.

Football remained his first love, however. In 1942, Palau left for the
military service, and at the age of twenty-nine Vince got his first head
coaching job. It paid $1,700 a year. Father Timothy Moore, a Carmelite
who had once been good enough to win a tryout with the Detroit Lions,
had arrived in 1941 to be the school's athletic director, and it was he
who hired Lombardi as Palau's successor, sweetening the offer by telling
him he could pick up a few extra dollars by teaching summer school. The
rest of the year, his coach's salary also required him to continue teaching Latin, physics, and chemistry.

Of St. Cecelia's four hundred students, about half were boys, not all
of whom were likely candidates for the football team. Father Moore was
a football enthusiast, however, and he not only encouraged Lombardi to
recruit talent for the team but also established a training camp near Hackettstown, New Jersey. It was not as well financed as those operated by
the pro teams, but the boys were ordered to report there each September 1, and when Lombardi was through with them they were ready for
the opening game or he knew the reason why.

Training camps for high school football were not customary, and
other coaches grumbled that St. Cecelia's was getting an unfair advantage. There was no rule against it in the parochial school league, however, and Father Tim ignored the complaints.

Lombardi ran into some more criticism from his rivals when he introduced the T formation, patterned on the offense used by the mighty
Chicago Bears. It was a new concept among Bergen County high school
teams, but it was well suited to his material, which consisted mostly of
boys who were small but fast. The innovation made them hard to beat.

Lombardi and Father Moore were sitting in the stands at a public
school championship game when they were approached by a coach from
a neighboring town.

"You two guys spoil football," he told them.

They accepted the compliment. If the T formation and the summer
camp were so unpopular with the enemy, obviously they must be pretty
good things to have.

Listening to Father Tim Moore reminisce about those days at St.
Cecelia's, a listener is struck by the consistency of Lombardi's methods
over the years. Even when he was hidden away in New Jersey, dealing

with high school boys at a time when some of his friends were important men in the ranks of the college coaches or with the pros, Vince was operating much as he did when his big chance finally came.

At the little parochial school in Englewood, trying to make players out of boys of fifteen or sixteen years old, he stressed football fundamentals, including careful conditioning and a willingness to accept discipline. His training camps near Hackettstown sound like the Packers' camps of the 1960s.

He had a low tolerance for error, then as later. He yelled a lot. His players feared his tongue and stepped warily to avoid his temper. But he produced winning teams. And as the coach's methods proved themselves, most of the boys developed a strong loyalty not only to the team but to the coach. Lombardi managed to get more out of his young players than they had known was in them, and with success came pride in the team and themselves.

"The one thing I require is a desire to play ball," the coach would tell each new group of boys. "Anybody who doesn't want to play, there's the door."

Such talk is common enough around athletic locker rooms, but somehow when Lombardi said it the words meant something. It was partly that the boys could sense that this intense young man meant every syllable. Vince said once that "football is a game of cliches, and I believe every one of them," which was no more or less than the truth.

No one left when he suggested that those who didn't want to give 100 percent effort head for the door, but some of the St. Cecelia's rookies soon wished they'd accepted the option offered. The coach drilled them to exhaustion. He shouted at them. Sometimes he shoved a lineman aside and took his place, demonstrating how to throw a block. He hit as hard as if he were still a Fordham Ram and the high school kid opposite him was a brawny guard from Pitt.

Getting blocked by Lombardi hurt, but there was no use complaining. The coach would just say, "Hurt is in the mind," the gospel handed down from Harry Lombardi.

Some of the boys grumbled among themselves. What the hell, they said, this wasn't pro ball, this was just high school and they weren't getting paid. The griping was done when the coach wasn't around but the word got back to him. He called the team together for a serious talk.

"You fellows think I work you too hard from Monday to Saturday," he said. "But it will make Sunday's game seem like a picnic."

Twenty years later, the Packers heard the same philosophy. As with the St. Cecelia's boys, they usually came around to the coach's way of thinking after it had been proved that the back-breaking training routine really did make them better players on Sunday afternoons.

Emotion was an integral part of football, Lombardi maintained, but sometimes his emotions got the better of him. Once he was having a shouting match in an office with a rival football coach when he lost his temper. He leaped over the desk, grabbed the man, and threw him onto a wastepaper basket. He cooled off as quickly as he'd flared up and apologized, and the men later became friends. But the story got around and it helped build Lombardi's reputation with the team and the townsfolk as a fellow to be treated with respect. The students felt the same mixture of fear and admiration for him as he was to arouse later in his career among players who outweighed the St. Cecelia's boys by a hundred pounds.

Even as a teacher, Lombardi inspired apprehension among his more timid pupils. Before school one morning, Father Moore was walking along the corridor when he saw a high school girl named Ruth crying. With a fatherly hand on her shoulder he asked what was wrong.

"My cousin was sick and I was staying with her and I'm supposed to go to Mr. Lombardi's class next and—"

"Slow down, Ruth. You're crying because your cousin's sick?"

"It's not that. I didn't get my homework done. I'm supposed to go to Mr. Lombardi's chemistry class, but I can't. I'm not going in that laboratory without my homework."

The priest knew that Ruth's family and the Lombardis were close friends and that Vince looked on the girl as almost a kid sister. He also knew that if she was supposed to have her homework and showed up without it, the friendship wouldn't make a bit of difference.

"Don't worry," he told her. "I'll go with you."

He knocked at the door. Lombardi opened it, blinking his eyes behind his glasses.

"What's the matter, what's the matter?" he demanded.

After Father Moore explained Ruth's problem, Lombardi said it would be all right. The door closed behind them and Father Moore heaved a sigh of relief. If Vince had heard about the missing homework before he understood the reason for it, the priest knew, Ruth would have been in a good deal of trouble.

Discipline was uncompromising in Lombardi's classes, but it was even stricter for the football players. During the school year, parents were responsible for the boys part of the day, but during the September football camps Vince could not only set the rules but also make sure they were enforced. Every Saturday night, he and Father Moore patrolled Hackettstown to make sure no player was breaking training.

The priest was especially worried about one of the players—a talented boy, but a mischief-maker. If Lombardi caught him fracturing a rule, he might kick him off the team. This would not only be hard on the lad but it would also make it tougher to win when the season started. Father Moore's scheme was to order the boy to stay at Lombardi's house on Saturday night so he wouldn't be tempted.

That solved that problem, but others arose. For example, when the star quarterback was caught smoking a cigarette, Lombardi didn't hesitate.

"Find out exactly when the next bus is coming," he told the boy. "Then get on it."

Father Moore is not only a kindly man but a practical one. He called the coach aside.

"Hey, Vince," he said. "Can't you overlook this? We need him."

Lombardi set his jaw.

"No, sir. If I do it for one, I'd have to do it for all."

The bus arrived. The ex-quarterback climbed glumly aboard. Lombardi wasn't there to watch him go. He was back on the field, yelling advice to his replacement.

The Lombardi system might not have worked with a losing team— no one knows for sure because Lombardi never had one. But when it paid off in victories, it was endurable. His first year at St. Cecelia's, his team won six, tied two, lost one—an excellent record but one that Vince claimed was not nearly good enough. To satisfy the coach, his players learned, their record should have been 9-0.

The next year they tried harder. His teams ran up an unbroken string of twenty-five victories over several seasons before Union Hill's boys tied St. Cecelia's. Then the team won six more victories before finally losing.

It was during this period of triumph when a high school boy named Reid Halahan saw the coach's wife standing on the side lines, watching practice. He walked over and made a complimentary comment about her husband.

"Some day," Marie Lombardi told him, "he'll be the next Knute Rockne."

Chapter 6

"A Rough Soul"

To his wife and some of the St. Cecelia's fans—perhaps even to himself, for he was not a man to downgrade his own abilities—Lombardi might have been another Rockne, but by 1946 he was thirty-three years old and his name meant nothing outside the neighborhood of Englewood, New Jersey.

He was making $3,500 a year as a high school coach and teacher. Some of the men he'd played with or against at Fordham were college coaches. Others were veteran players with the professional teams. Aware that Vince was getting restless, Father Moore got him a summer job with his brother, a contractor, figuring the extra money would help keep Lombardi from leaving St. Cecelia's.

Ray Moore paid him $102 a week and made him a foreman on a road-building project. Lombardi turned out to be the best foreman Moore had ever hired. Like Vince, most of the workmen were of Italian ancestry, and he was able to handle them well. He not only got more work out of them than Moore had believed possible, but he made them like it.

The problem at hand was the building of a portion of Highway 17 near the Lincoln Tunnel that connects Jersey with Manhattan. Lombardi plunged into the work with the same single-minded enthusiasm he brought to football. When the temporary employee's ten weeks were up, Moore took a look at the records of how much work his crew had done and told him he was wasting his time as a high school football coach.

"Work for me, Vince," Ray said. "You'll be making $40,000 a year in no time."

That was more money than Lombardi could make in ten years at the high school. He was tempted. But if he went with the construction firm, what would happen to his team now that the fall season was almost at hand?

"Thanks," he told Moore. "But I'll stick with football."

Moore could hardly believe that a man would make a decision like that, although his brother, Father Tim, was happy to hear about it. But another hazard was ahead for the athletic director of St. Cecelia's. It seemed that he was going to lose his coach to—perish the thought—a public high school.

Hackensack High was getting tired of losing to its small parochial neighbor. It was decided that if it couldn't beat Lombardi, maybe it could get him to join its ranks. The principal offered Vince $6,000 a year to coach the Hackensack football squad.

With a year to go on his contract with St. Cecelia's, Lombardi asked Father Moore if he could get out of it to accept this opportunity.

"Listen, you Mediterranean Irishman," Moore said, "if that's your ambition in life—to make $6,000 a year—then go ahead."

Hackensack was a bigger school. The material would be better. Recognition was more likely. But as soon as the word got out that Lombardi was leaving St. Cecelia's, the pressure mounted to get him to change his mind.

When his parents, who had moved to Englewood to live near their oldest son, heard he was leaving for a public school they would hardly speak to him. His kid brother, Joseph, was on the St. Cecelia's team, and he joined other members of the squad in pleading with the coach not to abandon them.

The boys wrote letters or stopped Vince on the street to plead with him. Women in the parish—the kind, Father Tim said "who don't know a football from a red apple"—urged him to change his mind. His friends at school pointed out that he'd been preaching loyalty, so how could he sell out to the enemy?

Finally Lombardi gave in. But he'd already told Hackensack High he'd take the job. He called on Moore.

"Father Tim you've got to get me out of this."

There was no use reaching a decision on an empty stomach. The priest met Vince at his parents' house. Matilda Lombardi set a large cheese on the table and most of it was gone by the time the conversation was over. Father Moore said he'd tell the newspaper that he'd refused to release the coach from his contract so he couldn't go to Hackensack.

The parish heaved a collective sigh of relief. Lombardi began to receive invitations to speak at spaghetti suppers and the like. When it came to such public appearances, Vince turned out to be surprisingly shy and ill at ease. Even at the Friday pep rally, facing an audience of high school students, he wasn't sure of himself.

"Write me out some jokes I can tell," he told Father Tim, and the priest obliged.

There was no such oratorical hanging back on the practice field or in the locker room. For one thing, jokes were not in order. Lombardi goaded and cajoled his boys as of old. And as before they kept on winning.

St. Cecelia's took the state parochial school championship six years out of seven. One year, his boys ran up a total of 267 points while allowing the opponents only 19. As Lombardi's reputation grew, other high schools besides Hackensack made him offers, but he had something else in mind. Fordham had dropped football in 1943, but according to the churchly grapevine it was going to revive it. Who would be a more logical choice of head coach than an alumnus who had proved himself the winningest coach in New Jersey?

Ed Danowski, it turned out. When football began again at the Rose Hill campus in 1946, Lombardi was ignored. Danowski had been a bigger star in college, but the decision hurt.

Ed was a big, easygoing fellow, popular with everyone on the campus. There was only one trouble—his team didn't win. In fact, Fordham lost all seven games that fall, including a 40-0 defeat by Louisiana State and a 68-0 disaster with Penn State. When the season ended, it was felt around Fordham that this had not been a distinguished debut for Danowski and it would be a good idea to get him some help.

So in 1947, at long last, Lombardi was back at Fordham. His task was to coach the freshmen and to recruit that year's crop of high school graduates. His St. Cecelia's background made him knowledgeable about where the potential talent was hidden in the New York area and his freshman squad went undefeated. The varsity did a little better, too. It tied New York University and won over King's Point. It lost the other six games, however, and in 1948 Lombardi was moved up a notch to be Danowski's assistant in charge of offense.

The end coach was Jim Lansing, who later became head coach. He had attended Fordham several years after Vince had graduated so they'd never met. Someone introduced them. Lombardi didn't even say hello.

He plunged immediately into a complicated diagram of a football play. Working for a team that had compiled a 1-1-13 record over the last two seasons, he felt there was no time to waste on the amenities.

By the time the recruits Lombardi had tracked down in 1947 were seniors, Fordham was no longer ashamed of its football team. It lost only to Yale that year, running up an 8-1 record. During 1948, Vince's first year in charge of the offense, the team that had averaged 6.3 points a game the previous season increased that figure to 20.2. Equally satisfying was the result of the NYU game. The Rams of '48 had won only two and lost six going into that contest, but after Lombardi had a little talk with them they whipped their old rivals by 26 to 0. It was a measure of revenge for that 1936 defeat that had kept the Seven Blocks of Granite from playing in the Rose Bowl.

Lombardi's talents soon impressed the Fordham football followers. There was talk that the wrong man was head coach. Ed Danowski was popular, however, and it seemed for a time that the campus would be split between two factions. Lombardi put a stop to the schism. Some of Danowski's detractors approached him and suggested that he try for Ed's job, but Vince turned them down. He felt some loyalty to his boss, but he felt even more to Fordham and had no intention of being the cause of a row, especially at time when a considerable body of opinion on the campus held that football should be dropped again.

Colleges were expanding rapidly, money was becoming scarce, and the Jesuits were thinking that football was a luxury that could be dispensed with. It became obvious to Lombardi that his old school was going to be only a temporary stopping place and he began to look around for another job. Among the friends he telephoned was Tim Cohane, the former college public relations man who was now a sportswriter.

Cohane knew of no job opening offhand, but a few days later he happened to meet Col. Earl Blaik on the way to a meeting in a Baltimore hotel. Blaik mentioned that Army was losing Sid Gilman, its line coach. Gilman had coached both offense and defense but two-platoon football was now in fashion and Blaik wanted to divide the job. He'd hired Murray Warmath to handle the defensive line but he still needed a man for offense.

Cohane suggested Lombardi.

"He's smart, tough, a hard worker, and a leader, Red. I think he's your kind of cat."

"Send him to me," the colonel ordered.

The coach of the New York Giants, Steve Owen, also mentioned Lombardi to Blaik as a likely candidate. Vince lost no time in driving up the Hudson to West Point where he and the colonel spent some time talking football and discussing coaching philosophy. A few days later, Cohane called Blaik.

"I hired Lombardi," the West Point coach told him. "He's right."

"What did you think of him?"

There was a pause while the colonel considered how to evaluate the character of his new assistant.

"He's a rough soul," he said finally.

Chapter 7

Victory and Scandal at West Point

Ever since the first soldiers marched off to war armed with clubs, military men have understood that an army that comes in second has not accomplished the job it has been given. Being a good loser wins few medals, and winning a war is usually considered even more important than winning a football game. So Lombardi's way and the Army way dovetailed in several important respects.

But the West Point coach was an admirer of Gen. Douglas MacArthur, and like him he felt that a war or a game should be conducted not only successfully but also with a flair. On the other hand, Lombardi didn't pay much attention to etiquette when it came to molding a winning team.

"Vince," Red Blaik would keep explaining to him, "we just don't do it that way at the Point. You can't talk to cadets that way."

Lombardi would try to remember the advice. But the next time an Army back zigged when he should have zagged, he'd dip into his Sheepshead Bay vocabulary again. The colonel hated to hear future officers and gentlemen called such names.

"He has a vile temper," he complained in discussing his new assistant. "He becomes profane on the field."

But it is hard to argue with success. Those future gentlemen in shoulder pads survived the invective and even took it to heart. They won nine games and lost none and soon Vince was promoted from coaching the offensive line to full responsibility for the offensive team.

If Lombardi influenced West Point football—and he did, often at the top of his voice—he was in turn influenced by it. For the first time since he'd left home, he had a father figure with whom he could identify. At St. Cecelia's, he had filled that role for the students. But now he became a follower as well as a leader, and the man he emulated was Red Blaik.

The colonel took MacArthur's motto, "There is no substitute for victory," and adapted it to the football field. Thus Lombardi was influenced by Blaik who was, in turn, influenced by the general; in both cases, however, the imitations were considerably short of slavish.

The young men in Lombardi's charge at West Point were ideal material for his methods. They were trained to take orders without questioning them and to accept discipline as a matter of course. Perhaps without knowing it, Vince had been seeking just such military discipline for years, so the Army suited him fine.

Lombardi kept trying to fit in with the protocol accepted at West Point. He made a habit of calling each player "mister" so he wouldn't call him something less complimentary—a custom he was to carry over to Green Bay and Washington with his hired hands there. But when things went wrong, his language and tone of voice were apt to be more suited to a Fort Dix top sergeant than to a civilian speaking to future officers of the United States Army.

Blaik, in his gentlemanly way, kept suggesting his assistant lower the decibels and choose more dignified adjectives. But when someone missed a block or fumbled the ball, Lombardi forgot that the culprit might some day become chief of staff.

Walking downwind from the practice field, some of the West Point brass were inclined to wince at Lombardi's choice of descriptions of the Army football players. But the season was climaxed by trouncing Navy 39 to 0, and no one at the Point was opposed to a triumph of truth and justice like that. As for Blaik and most of the players, they learned to respect and eventually to admire this loud and emotional fellow from Brooklyn who took football with such unswerving seriousness. Before long, Blaik was showing him off in the Union League Club, confident that Lombardi would not forget himself and raise his voice to the point where he'd wake up those members dozing in the overstuffed chairs. The colonel even entrusted him with the high honor of taking the game films to the Waldorf Tower, which was now serving as MacArthur's dugout.

As a living monument, it would have been unseemly for the general to visit the stadium very often in person. Even for his hero, Blaik couldn't move the games to the Waldorf lobby—for one thing, it had no goal posts or chalk lines So the next best thing was to send films of Army's games to the Tower bivouac, and it was a mark of Red Blaik's confidence in Lombardi that he sometimes entrusted him with this mission.

The general was a West Pointer with a warm spot in his heart for the Army team, particularly an Army team that could whip the current representatives of the Navy. During World War II, MacArthur and the admirals had seldom seen eye to eye, and it was no more than simple justice that Annapolis should be trounced soundly each fall.

And so they met, the old hero of the Pacific, the future hero of Green Bay. It is pleasant to think of them there, high above Park Avenue, engrossed in the spectacle of last week's triumph while a projector flickered respectfully in the background. No recording was made of their meetings, but the odds are at least six to five that Lombardi told the general about football and MacArthur explained military tactics to the wholesale butcher's son.

Lombardi did not agree with the old warhorse's politics. Vince was a Democrat, and the general, although he once made a halfhearted try for the Republican nomination for president, was essentially a Whig. But the coach admired the general's grasp of tactics—a military campaign and a football season had certain surface similarities—and it is safe to say that each, in his own way, was impressed with the other.

Their first meeting was in Japan. MacArthur was running the Korean War at the time, having finished straightening out the Japanese, and the Army coaching staff was on an off-season trip to bolster morale. It brought along the filmed highlights of the previous fall's games. As Army had gone unbeaten, the commanding general enjoyed them very much.

It was during Vince's first year at West Point that Blaik's team played Fordham, with both teams having won all their previous games. This gave the sportswriters a chance to claim that the game was for the championship of the East, because football is played only on weekends as a rule and sportswriters have to write something for the paper every day. A considerable number of the Rams' players had been recruited by Lombardi while he was at Fordham, but now his loyalty was to Army, and until after the final whistle they represented the enemy.

The Fordham team had scored 166 points in winning the season's first four games, allowing the opposition only 43. But Army whipped the Rams by a score of 35 to 0. It was not a close game, but it was a rough and sometimes bloody one. Afterward it led to a shouting match between

Lombardi and his old friend Tim Cohane, each contending that the opposition had started the rough stuff. The Irish and Italian tempers hit boiling point, and a bystander might have supposed that the men would forever be mortal enemies.

Actually, both forgot the argument almost as soon as it was over, and Lombardi was soon helping the sportswriter pick a mythical All-American team named after a West Point landmark. The Bull Pond All-America included such players as Chuckles Axemurder of Bedlam Hall and Excalibur Slime of King Arthur's Knight School. The selection became an annual custom and some years later Lombardi told Cohane that his all-time favorites on the Bull Pond squad were Ugh, the Carlisle guard, and Oscar Upchuck of Old Nausea.

"It took a great deal of thought to pick Oscar Upchuck over Heinrich Schnorkel of Underwasser University," Vince wrote to his friend. "I guess, however, l have always had a soft spot in my heart for good old Upchuck."

Lombardi's early West Point years were among the happiest of his life. He even managed to forget football long enough to play golf—he had seldom taken time for it at St. Cecelia's or Fordham—although playing golf with Vince was seldom sheer relaxation. He worked as hard at winning this game as any other, and his agony when his ball bounced into the rough was painful to see.

He picked up some new axioms. A favorite saying of Colonel Blaik's was, "If you can walk, you can run." Lombardi took its meaning quite literally. The time came when various hamstrung football players got very tired of hearing it.

It was at West Point that Lombardi and Col. O. C. Krueger became friends and golfing companions. Ockie Krueger later became commandant of Fort Meade, Maryland. When he was getting close to retirement, he got a call from Vince, who by then was in charge of the Packers. The Packers needed a man to run their office in Milwaukee, where a portion of Green Bay's home games were then played. Krueger accepted the job. Later, when Lombardi moved to the Redskins, the colonel followed him to Washington. It was typical of Vince that he kept the friendship going. Becoming Lombardi's friend was not easy—he maintained a reserve that was sometimes criticized, especially in the free and easy atmosphere of a small city in Wisconsin. But once a man had been accepted fully, he was his friend for life.

The pleasant life at West Point continued through the 1950 season, with the Army team once again riding high. It ended in late summer of 1951. Until then, another successful season seemed certain. But after the cribbing scandal broke, there was a serious question of whether West Point would have a football team at all.

All but two of the juniors and seniors on the team had to leave the cadet corps. They were among ninety young men who were forced out of the academy for cheating. Some of them had been guilty only of putting friendship above the West Point code of conduct and had merely failed to report knowledge that others had accepted help with their examinations.

The situation arose from the fact that various cadets had the same classes on different days. If one of them brought a copy of an exam from the classroom, others who took the same class later in the week could learn the questions in advance. The football players were particularly vulnerable to the benefits of this practice. They had to combine a full scholastic schedule with practice and out-of-town trips, which meant they were sometimes in desperate need of shortcuts. Their friends were often equally anxious to keep the players eligible for future games.

Among those caught up in the cribbing scandal was Red Blaik's son, Bob, the team's quarterback. Apparently young Blaik had not accepted help himself, but he had failed to turn informer as the code required. The colonel was so bitter about the situation that he seriously considered resigning. He felt that the brass had failed to take into consideration the fact that such cribbing had gone on for years and was virtually a tradition—though admittedly, not one of the Point's traditions anyone bragged about much. He implied that the fact that Gen. George C. Marshall, then Secretary of Defense and the man with the ultimate authority, had not gone to West Point had something to do with the severity of the punishment.

In this crisis, Blaik conferred with his mentor at the Waldorf. MacArthur was sympathetic. He said the scandal should never have been allowed to become known outside the academy walls. The way to have handled it, he suggested, would have been for the ringleaders to be given "a kick in the pants" and the others let off with a reprimand.

But the general had no influence with President Truman, the man who'd fired him after he was accused of mixing politics with military tactics during the Korean War, and the ninety cadets were dismissed by presidential decree after being refused a chance to bring their cases before a court martial.

Blaik had been offered a $50,000 job elsewhere, but MacArthur talked him out of taking it. It was his duty to stay on the firing line, Red was told. So with the season almost upon them the colonel and his assistants had to create a team out of the ragged remnants of the material the departures had left them.

The 1950 Army team had ranked second nationally. The quality of the players who were lost is indicated by the fact that in the pro draft of 1953 eleven former cadets who continued their educations at other schools were picked.

With the opening game with Villanova looming close, Lombardi as offensive coach had to try to build an attack around a third string quarterback, an inexperienced line, and a fullback who weighed 152 pounds. He'd had plenty of backs at St. Cecelia's who weighed more than that.

There was talk of calling off the season, but Blaik and his aides grimly went ahead. Somehow, Army got past its opener but Northwestern was next. Lombardi cajoled and threatened. He wore out his chalk going over and over diagrams of simple plays. He appealed to the cadets' pride. He convinced at least some of them that they belonged on the field in a game against a Big Ten team. For a while, it seemed as if the extraordinary efforts would pay off.

With only a few seconds to play, Northwestern was behind. Watching the clock, Vince felt that a victory for Army would somehow vindicate Blaik and restore the tarnished reputation of the venerable institution on the Hudson.

But Northwestern's quarterback faded back and threw a desperation pass. A more experienced defender might have batted it down, but the ball was caught and Army failed to stop the score.

When the season was over, West Point had lost seven and won only two. Looking back on it, a memory stood out in the mind of Col. Red Blaik; the sight of his tough offensive coach standing on the sidelines after the Northwestern game had ended, tears running down his face.

In their time of trouble, Blaik and Lombardi's friendship grew closer. Much of the enjoyment of being at West Point had vanished for both of them, but Vince felt this was no time to leave a man he admired in the lurch and look for opportunities elsewhere. Though not content with being number two man, even when number one was the colonel, he stayed on.

After the difficult autumn of 1951, Vince continued as Army's offensive coach for two more seasons, helping rebuild the team's reputation. After the 1953 season, Steve Owen decided to retire as coach of the New York Giants. Blaik was offered the job but turned it down. What they needed, he told the Giants' officials, was a younger man, a more ambitious man, someone with a reputation still to make. As a matter of fact, he said, he knew just the man—someone who would fit in well with the kind of football played by the professionals.

Blaik didn't have to tell Wellington Mara, one of the Giants owners, about Lombardi, his Fordham classmate. The front office gave due consideration to the Army coach's recommendation, but it was decided that the Giants needed a more prominent name. As far as the general public was concerned, Lombardi was unknown. Who pays any attention to assistant coaches?

Pro football was still struggling for fan support. Guaranteed sellouts for every Sunday afternoon were still in the future. So were the days of lucrative television contracts. Besides, Vince's only professional experience had been with a minor league team and his only chance at a head coaching job had been at a small parochial high school.

So Jim Lee Howell got the job. Vincent Lombardi was forty years old and somehow, when it came to the important jobs, he was always passed by. By the time Knute Rockne was forty, he'd been Notre Dame's coach for ten years. If Vince was going to fulfill his wife's prediction of some years back and become a second Rockne, somebody somewhere was going to have to give him a chance to show what he could do.

Chapter 8

In the Pros but Not in Charge

When that genial Arkansas gentleman named Jim Lee Howell took over the New York Giants after the 1953 season, it was obvious he could use all the help he could get. The team had won only three of its last twelve games, and all but the most dedicated fans were toying with such emotions as disinterest and disenchantment. Even worse, it was getting harder to sell tickets.

Soon after he became coach, Howell sat down with the owners to discuss who would be hired to assist him. He wanted Allie Sherman as his offensive coach, but Sherman was upset over Owen's departure and turned down the job.

"Well, what about Lombardi?" Wellington Mara asked.

"I don't know if I want him or not," Howell said. "But we could talk about it."

When the word reached Vince that he was under consideration, he wasn't sure whether he wanted Howell, either. But he was willing enough to talk, even though he had to travel all the way to Jim Lee's farm in Lonoke, Arkansas, before the conversation could begin. Lonoke didn't look at all like Sheepshead Bay or even Manhattan, but when the talk got started it was mostly about football and Lombardi was willing to discuss that subject anywhere, including Arkansas.

The big, easygoing Howell and his shorter, more intense visitor spent the entire weekend jawing about football in general and the sorry state of the Giants in particular. When the talk ended, they'd decided they could get along with each other and Vince was hired. It had been a long time since he'd taken the subway from Brooklyn to watch the professionals play, but at last he was one of them.

"I don't want any yes-men around here," Jim Lee announced, which was fortunate. Neither Lombardi, who was in charge of the offense, nor Tom Landry, the defensive coach, fell into that comfortable category. Lombardi was a man of many words, Landry a man of few, but "yes, boss," was an unlikely combination of syllables to come from either of them.

Howell soon was satisfied that he'd chosen well. He considered both of his assistants brilliant football men and gave them a relatively free hand. The system worked well, but that didn't mean it always worked smoothly.

"It's like getting along with your wife," Howell said, in reminiscing about life with Landry and Lombardi. "You love her, but sometimes things come up you don't agree on."

One of the perpetual arguments resulted from the impossibility of fitting two sixty-minute practice sessions into a ninety minute period. Howell felt that practice ought to last ninety minutes, and neither of his assistants disagreed. But Lombardi wanted sixty of those minutes to work on offense, and Landry wanted the same amount of time for defense.

Lombardi made more noise about it, but Landry, who would become Vince's perennial rival as coach of the Dallas Cowboys, made his points just as firmly. Howell let the arguments bounce off him and worked out a compromise. With each of the assistant trying to cram sixty minutes of instruction into forty-five minutes, the Giants gradually took on the look of a winning football team.

When he first arrived, Vince had things to learn. The pros' game was different from the kind played by the college boys he had coached at West Point or Fordham. Lombardi's background on the running game was sound enough and this remained his favorite way of advancing the ball. But he had things to learn about the uses of the forward pass. At first, Frank Gifford and some of the other veterans were explaining things to him.

As at St. Cecelia's when he'd been made a basketball coach, he listened respectfully to anyone who seemed to know what he was talking about. He studied the players and their talents. Soon he had grasped the fine points of the professional game and was adapting them to his own way of doing things.

He required no advice from the old pros when it came to dealing with another Giants tradition, that of hearing suggestions on coaching matters from some members of the front office. Lombardi was a new man in the ranks, but he would tolerate no such interference. He instructed one of his bosses, Wellington Mara, in how things would be run.

"When I have a meeting with my unit, I don't want any outsiders present," he told him, leaving no doubt that when he said "outsiders" he meant the team brass.

"I'm going to have to criticize. I have to feel free to criticize in my own way. I don't want any outsiders to hear that criticism. I don't want any of the players humiliated by having outsiders hear that criticism."

Mara said that was fine with him. Lombardi was able to speak freely to the hired hands, and did. He approached his new responsibility with confidence and single-minded enthusiasm. He got the power sweep going, the ball carrier following a muscular escort around the end of the line. He introduced the Giants to Red Blaik's version of the belly series. He drilled the players over and over on the same play until it seemed certain they would do it right on Sunday, when it counted. But perfection sometimes eluded them.

One week, he spent several hours working with a promising rookie, an end, trying to get him to run exactly the proper pattern without having to think about it. By Thursday, the young man was doing it right. It gave Lombardi considerable satisfaction.

But then, in the last practice before the game, the play was called and the end ran it wrong. Vince gave a bellow of frustration and rage. He charged out onto the field. The rookie took one look at him, then ran for his life.

No one ever found out what the coach would have done to the young man if he caught him. The end might have a short attention span when it came to play patterns, but he could run faster than the former Block of Granite. Lombardi finally cooled down and gave up the chase. It wasn't so much that the kid had made a stupid mistake, he told Howell later. What made him lose his temper was that the rookie hadn't seemed sorry enough about it.

The power sweep—it became famous as the Green Bay sweep some years later—was one of Lombardi's favorite plays even while he was with the Giants. He considered it a beautiful way to advance the ball, each blocker fulfilling his assignment, the ball carrier protected by a moving wall of muscular young men. It was not a complicated play but,

Lombardi kept explaining over and over, there was a right way to do it and a wrong way. The right way, the players soon learned, could also be referred to as the Lombardi way.

He collected movies of a succession of such plays. He ran the film repeatedly for his offensive squad, patiently pointing out why the play worked one time, how it was botched the next. When they were thoroughly sick of the film he switched on the lights and went to the blackboard, diagraming the play so it could be understood by a moderately alert kindergartener. But this still wasn't enough.

"Out on the field," he'd order, and then he would have these well-paid athletes walk through the power sweep, then jog through it, and finally, when he was at last satisfied that each knew what to do, run through it at full speed.

Such painstaking methods came in for some criticism—after all, the sweep was a simple and rather old-fashioned way to advance the ball, not some startling tactical invention. But Lombardi believed that it would be effective only if the players practiced it enough, understood it thoroughly, and believed in it.

As practical men, the players had to admit that the Lombardi methods got results. In 1953, the Giants had scored a total of 179 points in 12 games. In 1954, his first season as the team's offensive coach, they scored 293, increasing their average from slightly over two touchdowns a game to three touchdowns and a field goal. Even more convincing was the fact that they won seven games that season, four more than in 1953.

Under Landry, the defensive team was also improving. New York had not won a National Football League championship since 1938, but in 1956 it took the title. As head coach, Howell had the basic responsibility and was entitled to claim the credit, but Jim Lee was generous about pointing out that he had the two finest assistants in football. A number of outside observers were inclined to agree, and Lombardi had hope that he would at last be tapped for a head coaching job elsewhere.

Tim Cohane was among those who felt he deserved a chance to run the show. The sportswriter suggested his old friend's name to officials of the Air Force Academy, Notre Dame, and Southern California, but no offer came. Lombardi began to wonder if one ever would.

In California for the Rose Bowl game on New Year's Day of 1957, the two men had dinner together.

"I know I can coach," Vince told him, for they knew each other well enough that he could speak frankly about his disappointment. "I know it, but the right people never seem to know it.

"I'm forty-three now. I'm not getting any younger. Maybe I'll never get my chance."

Lombardi was not only talking like a man who expected no more opportunities to open to him but he was also acting like one. Prepared to stay on indefinitely as an assistant coach in New York, he bought a house at Fairhaven, New Jersey, near his relatives and his wife's relatives and not far from his old friends at Englewood. He even purchased a family burial plot in a Fairhaven cemetery. The children, Vincent and Susan, were growing up, and it seemed that this was the town where the family might settle for good.

But then came the kind of offer he'd been waiting for—a delegation from the Philadelphia Eagles' front office arrived and said they wanted him as head coach.

"For how long?"

"We'll give you a two-year contract."

But now that the chance had arrived, Lombardi refused to jump at it. The Eagles' record indicated a long rebuilding process would be necessary. He wanted to coach, but he knew that if he got the reputation as a loser he might never get a second chance.

"I need five years," he told them. "I can't settle for less than a five-year contract."

The Philadelphians offered to compromise with a three-year deal, but because the Eagles were the worst team in the league except for the Green Bay Packers, Vince insisted on five years or nothing.

So it was nothing, and when the fall arrived he was still Jim Lee Howell's assistant. A few other offers had come his way, but they were from colleges that were too small or where football was being de-emphasized.

In 1958, the Giants won the Eastern Division title and, in a game that fans still talk about, played the Baltimore Colts for the league championship. Tied at the end of the fourth quarter, the teams continued in overtime and the Giants lost 23-17.

Although his team had lost, Lombardi got his share of the spotlight. The off-season rumors began, with Vince's name cropping up in discussions of coaching jobs. There was one he might have taken—Red Blaik had retired and Army was looking for a successor. But that offer did not come. Perhaps the brass still remembered that Colonel Blaik's former assistant was not quite the West Point type.

The bid for Lombardi's services came from a point farther west. Lombardi had never seen Green Bay, Wisconsin, but when the Packers' executive committee invited him to fly out and have a talk he climbed aboard a plane.

When the meeting was over, one of the first persons he called was the man who'd given him his head coaching job at St. Cecelia's. He told Father Moore he'd been offered the job of not only coaching the Packers but also being the team's general manager. He would have full authority to run things, he said, and he was going to accept.

"How long is the contract for, Vince?" the priest asked.

"Five years."

"Don't take it. Ask them for a two-year contract. Howell is about to retire. If you tie yourself up for five years, you'll never get back to New York."

"They won only one game out of twelve last year."

"I know, but—"

"Listen, Tim. I've got to have five years. It might take me two years to win a game. Then nobody will want me."

When the word got out that an assistant coach named Vincent T. Lombardi was to be Green Bay's coach and general manager, the less knowledgeable fans said, "Lombardi? What'd he ever do?" And the more philosophical followers said, "At least the Pack can't do much worse."

Only by losing twelve out of twelve regular season games could the team Lombardi was to take over compile a more discouraging record than it had in 1958. A time was to come in professional football when even such a collection of losers might have packed stadiums, but that era was still a few years off. As it was, a fan could decide ten minutes before game time that it was a pleasant day to watch the Pack struggle with their betters, hop in the car, stop at the ticket window, and buy as many seats as he could afford. Capacity crowds were unusual in those days when the Packers were playing, and a serious question was being raised about whether the team would survive.

To be fair about it, it probably would have—even if the offer to Lombardi had not been made, even if the team went on losing eleven out of twelve games a season. The change in pro football's fortunes during the decade to come was due partly to television, partly to good times that left spare money for luxuries like football tickets. Some of the change can be credited to Lombardi and his influence on the game, but there is no use pretending that if he had turned in his uniform and gone into some other line of work football would have become a minor sport like squash. As for Green Bay, it's hard to imagine what would have happened to that small city's chances of survival in a league meant for large cities. But it had survived numerous crises in the past, and even without the man who became known as its resident miracle worker it may well have muddled through.

The team went back to a pickup group that had won ten games in 1919, then lost the season finale to an outfit from another Wisconsin city that called itself by the unlikely name of the Beloit Fairies. Green Bay's representatives chose a more appropriate name—at least, it was appropriate at the time because a local packing house had kicked in enough money for uniforms.

In 1921, the Packers joined what developed into the National Football League. They competed against teams from cities in Green Bay's population class or somewhat larger—Decatur, Akron, Canton, Dayton, Rock Island, Rochester, and Columbus—along with those from a few larger metropolises. It is a pretty good indication of pro football's financial status in those days that the Columbus team called itself the Panhandlers.

It has been said that the Packers staggered through those early years like a hungover fullback with a muscle pull, but the other cities' representatives were no better off. The Decatur, Illinois, team survived by moving to Chicago and becoming the Bears. Other NFL teams came and went. But Green Bay hung on, mostly because of a young man named Earl Lambeau and the rest of a committee known as the Hungry Five.

Curly Lambeau was the coach, the manager, the head fund raiser, the public relations man, and, not quite coincidentally, the best ball carrier on the club. His highest paid regular made ends meet by working as a Boy Scout director. Any fan who was willing to pay five dollars and buy six season tickets could become a part owner of the Packers. Even at this modest price, the response was underwhelming.

The team survived partly on local pride and the support of a small but stubborn contingent of dedicated fans. But the Green Bay team was no worse off than some others in the league. There was a time in the early twenties when the Giants franchise in the nation's biggest city was worth exactly $500.

Green Bay finished second to those bargain-priced Giants in 1927 and two years later won its first NFL championship. The players included Cal Hubbard, Mike Michalske, and a young man from Pottsville, Pa., John McNally, better known by the flamboyant alias of Johnny Blood.

In 1930, the team added Arnie Herber, a star whose memory is still green along the banks of the Fox River. Thanks to this halfback who could throw a sixty-yard forward pass, the Packers won their second title that year. It became the first team in history to win three in a row by repeating in 1931.

But while Wisconsin football fans, like those elsewhere, preferred watching a winner, most of them couldn't afford to buy tickets. In the midst of history's worst depression, going to football games was a luxury to men who were worrying about how to keep food on the family table. The team struggled through a disappointing season in 1932, a year when disappointments were not uncommon. Then in 1933, it went into bankruptcy. The immediate cause was a court decision awarding damages to a fan who had been injured.

That should have been that—by now it was being widely said that no city of Green Bay's size belonged in a major league. But Lambeau was not ready to give up and neither were the other members of the Hungry Five. With its financial affairs patched together somehow, in 1936 the Packers were back on top of the league, riding there on the skills of such players as Don Hutson, Cecil Isbell, and Clarke Hinkle. It also won titles in 1939 and 1944, but with the end of World War II professional football moved into an era of bigger budgets, and the smallest city in the league found the competition increasingly tough.

The All-America Conference was organized and began bidding against the NFL for players. Lambeau was still coach, but his executive committee had expanded to thirteen persons, leading to intramural bickering behind the scenes. If the team had kept on winning, things might have been different, but in 1947 it recorded only six victories, losing five and tying one. This was considered quite disappointing, but it turned out to be Lambeau's last winning season and the best record the team compiled before the Lombardi era began.

Bankruptcy loomed again in 1949, when the Packers won two and lost ten. It was avoided only by making enough money to pay the most pressing bills with receipts from an intrasquad benefit game. The situation was so serious that winter that Lambeau gave up his usual custom of heading for California to dodge Wisconsin's snow and cold, but even this personal sacrifice wasn't enough. He lost his fight to retain control of the club and resigned.

After thirty-one years under one coach, the Packers tried three in the next eight years. A former Chicago Bears halfback named Gene Ronzani lasted four seasons, a period in which the only commodity in oversupply was advice. Despite all that helpful nagging by some of the executive committeemen, the players kept losing more games than they won, and in 1954 it was decided to give Lisle Blackbourn a chance.

Liz Blackbourn, who had been born in a Wisconsin hamlet named Beetown, had done well as a high school coach, then made a reputation at Marquette University before it decided to drop football. After he switched to the Packers, the team managed to win only four of its twelve games, but the consensus among football men was that Liz had done remarkably well with the material available. In fact, he came within one vote of winning the "Coach of the Year" title over Paul Brown, which shows how outsiders felt about the skill it required to win even four games with the players then wearing Green Bay uniforms.

In 1955, the team responded to Blackbourn's coaching by winning six and losing six and seemed to be on its way back to respectability. But the 1956 and 1957 seasons can only be described as disasters, which is why Ray McLean was hired to replace Liz in 1958.

Scooter McLean was an optimistic man and, judging from his preseason prediction, a foolhardy one.

"We're going for the title," he announced. He didn't go so far as to say they'd win it, you understand, and it could be argued that every team is going for the title, at least until after the end of the first game. Still it was a prediction McLean lived to regret.

The Packers of 1958 did have one notable distinction. By winning one game, tying one, and losing ten, they became the worst team in the Packers' long history in the league. Long before the final game of that season had dragged its way into the record books, the feeling around Green Bay was that at least three things were needed: more money, better players, and a new coach.

The first two would be hard to get. As for the third, McLean was told his first season with the Packers was his last, and the executive committeemen started listening to suggestions about who should be his successor.

"Get Lombardi," NFL Commissioner Bert Bell advised. "Lombardi's the one you need," said Paul Brown, the resident football genius of the Cleveland Browns.

And so they got Lombardi and the days of being a poor country cousin at the NFL table were about to end.

Chapter 9

At Last, Vince to the Rescue

And it came to pass that after Vincent Lombardi descended out of the skies—that is, he flew in from New York—he lost no time in getting his bearings.

Before he had been in Green Bay twelve hours he had hired two assistant coaches—Phil Bengston and Red Cochran; submitted to numerous interviews with a patience that did not prove inexhaustible; helped his wife rent a house; begun preparations to sign the team's first draft choice; dealt with miscellaneous decisions involving the front office; and, by no means least important, given his nominal bosses a valuable lesson on how to conduct themselves in his vicinity. And thus passed the morning and the evening of the first day and Lombardi rested.

The lesson in deportment took place at the Green Bay airport, with an emphatic postscript added shortly afterward. The stage had been set some days earlier, when Lombardi was holding a hastily called press conference at a New York hotel to discuss his new job. While it was going on, Vince was interrupted by a telephone call from a small upstate Wisconsin radio station. Would the new coach take time for a brief airport interview when he arrived in Green Bay?

"Sure," Lombardi said, then went back to finish explaining to the Manhattan sportswriters why he'd decided to leave the Giants:

"I knew it was time to make a move if I ever was going to make one. It's a challenge."

He signed his contract on January 28, 1959. A few days later, he boarded the plane for Green Bay. Several members of the Hungry Five were there to welcome him along with a delegation of other important men. As they started to lead him away, a young man carrying a tape recorder tugged at his sleeve. He'd been promised an interview, he explained, but he got short shrift from the entourage—this was not the proper time to bother Vince, he was told, but there'd be a press conference later.

The voice explaining the brush-off was not Lombardi's, however, and so, it was quickly made obvious, the decision was of no value whatsoever.

"I promised this man an interview," the coach said. "So he's going to get it."

If there had been any disposition to argue, it was abandoned when the important men took a second look at the firm set of Lombardi's jaw. The interview went forward, lasting exactly as long as Vince wanted it to last and not a second longer, and the executive committeemen waited.

This was their first real taste of life with Lombardi. But he had once been a high school teacher, so he knew that to be fully assimilated a lesson should be repeated. An hour or two later, he explained to the club's board of directors exactly what their proper role would be.

"I want it understood," he said, "that I'm in complete command."

That was strong talk for a man just starting his first head coaching assignment in the pros at the age of forty-five. Some of the men he was putting in their place could have pointed out that without their efforts there would have been no Green Bay team for this arrogant outsider to come storming in from New York to coach. Not since the early days of Curly Lambeau had the Packers been under the total control of one man.

Not since then had the club been a winner. Around Green Bay, both on and off the executive committee, it was hoped that these two facts were not going to prove a mere coincidence.

By grasping all the authority, the new coach and general manager had also grabbed the responsibility for restoring the team to both respectability in the standings and solvency at the box office. He had already cut off his line of retreat. There would be no one else to blame if things went wrong.

Lombardi had been around football all his adult life, and he knew what would happen if the Packers failed to win. As a new man in town, he could expect that the fans would give him a few months to show what he could do. But unless the team's improvement was obvious by then, the wolves would gather and begin to howl.

True, he had a five-year contract. It seemed doubtful that the Packers could afford to pay him off and boot him out while its terms were valid even if his coaching proved no more triumphal than Scooter McLean's. On the other hand, a couple more 1-10-1 seasons and those hands that were slapping his back now would be pulling on the rope to hang him in effigy from a Green Bay lamppost. He had put himself out on a limb as soon as he signed his contract, he had crawled out still farther when he emphasized that he was in complete command, and he was perched there all by himself.

It was now the month of February, a month when Wisconsin's weather is always at its most bracing. The season was seven months away, the ground was hidden under a foot or two of snow the thermometer kept sagging downward below the zero mark. Even around Green Bay, which has more football addicts per square foot than any other community in the world, February is not the ideal time to think of forward passes, blocks, and tackles. But Lombardi plunged into his new job as if opening day was tomorrow afternoon.

Having completed the most pressing chores during his first twelve hours in his new job, he was back at work on the second day. Or was he?

"If you want Mr. Lombardi," visitors to his office were told, "you'll have to wait. He's watching movies."

But the film he was watching did not star John Wayne or even that TV cartoon character who was one of his favorites, Yogi Bear. It involved a number of young men wearing Packer uniforms. The coach did not write down his critique of the production, but it is certain he did not enjoy it very much.

These were the players he had inherited, and he did not like the way they blocked, tackled, kicked, ran, or threw and vainly pursued the forward pass. He did not like the way they fumbled, snapped the ball, sat on the bench, or ran on and off the field. Most of all, he did not like the statistics that accompanied the films of last season's disasters, particularly those which indicated that Green Bay had given up 393 points to opponents in twelve games while scoring 193. When he was teaching at St. Cecelia's his specialties had been chemistry, physics, and Latin rather than mathematics, but it was not hard to figure out that when a team scores an average of 16.08 points a game and allows its enemies to score 32.75, it is unlikely to win very often.

Crouched there in the darkness, the projector flickering inexorably onward, Lombardi found that the movie's most painful sequence dealt with a midseason game between the Packers and the Baltimore Colts. Let us not dwell on the details. The final score is enough. The Colts scored 56 points that afternoon and the Packers scored none. It was hard to believe that any professional team could lose by a score of 56 to 0, but it had happened, he could see the evidence unrolling before his eyes, and these were the players who would make or break Lombardi, a man who was approaching his forty-sixth birthday without having accomplished very much that would be remembered in the world of sports. It was reason to wonder if he'd made a mistake in coming to this frozen northland instead of staying in New York and waiting for Jim Lee Howell to get tired of coaching the Giants.

It was during this period of gloomy evaluation of his chances that one of his bosses—his nominal bosses, that is, a member of the executive committee—arrived to see him, first calling ahead and making an appointment.

"What do you want to talk about?" Vince asked as soon as the boss walked in.

"I just want to talk about the organization."

"I don't have time to just talk," Lombardi said, and that was the end of the conference.

Such an attitude struck some Green Bay residents as not only abrupt but unnecessarily abrasive. But as far as the coach and general manager of the Packers was concerned, he'd merely stated an obvious truth.

Watching the game films, Lombardi realized that for a man who'd always been associated with winners he was now in the unhappy position of being surrounded by losers.

The team had placed last in the Western Division in 1958, a result attained strictly on merit. On the other hand, in the after-hours league of the historic Fox River Valley, some of the players had established records that may stand forever.

It was part of Lombardi's teachings that a man must play with abandon, and they had done so. Not on the football field perhaps, but elsewhere. When such bachelors as Paul Hornung and Max McGee were described enviously as swingers, their fans weren't talking about how they moved across the enemy's twenty-yard line.

On the pre-Lombardi football team those players who did not swing were inclined to brood. If a team can't beat anyone but Philadelphia, it seemed logical to choose one philosophy or the other—moody introspection or gay forgetfulness. The only other choice was to take up another line of work and this had been considered, too. Hornung and Bart Starr, among others, had given this possibility serious attention.

The fact that he had been picked 199th in the draft had not helped build Starr's self-confidence. Even more discouraging were the long afternoons he spent on the bench while other quarterbacks—and not very successful quarterbacks, at that—were trying to guide the Packers toward the distant enemy goal line. Starr had a lot of time to think things over during that endless season of 1958, and his prospects were not encouraging. Even after Lombardi arrived, Starr remained a second stringer, with Lamar McHan given what seemed like a firm grip on the quarterback's spot.

Hornung's case was somewhat different. He had been one of the most heralded draft choices when he joined the Pack, having established an enviable reputation at Notre Dame, on the field as well as off. But now, except in the Fox River Valley after-hours league, he was considered a disappointment.

His coaches had never quite known what to do with such a talented young man. He could run with a ball, pass it, or kick it, and they hadn't been able to decide whether he was a quarterback, halfback, fullback, or kicker. Under his brash exterior, Hornung was equally confused about where he belonged, or whether he belonged in professional football at all.

Lombardi lost no time in informing him that he was a halfback. Hornung believed him and before long no one in the NFL doubted that the Golden Boy was a halfback and one of the best who ever wore a uniform.

"Inside the twenty-yard line," Vince was to say of him, "he's the greatest player around."

He still handled some of the kicking chores and occasionally he threw a pass, but mostly he carried the ball as co-leader with Jim Taylor of Green Bay's ground game. He felt, with considerable justice, that the new coach had rescued him from the curse of his own versatility. As for Lombardi, he took a special, almost fatherly interest in this handsome blond athlete who had the admirable talent of playing best when the stakes were highest.

The coach tried hard not to play favorites. Of the countless evaluations of his methods that were made over the years, Henry Jordan's remark on this subject was the most widely quoted.

"He's fair," the big lineman said. "He treats us all alike—like dogs."

But there was a special spark between Hornung and Lombardi. Something in Vince's complex psyche was attracted to a player who seemed to be the coach's antithesis.

Lombardi was a religious man, a family man. Hornung's attitude was typified by a piece of advice he said he'd once been given by his father: "Never get married in the morning or it'll spoil your whole day." Lombardi believed in discipline, particularly self-discipline. Hornung sometimes flouted the rules. Lombardi took football very seriously. So did Hornung, while he was on the field, but not always when the game was over.

Considering Lombardi's background, it is possible to speculate that Hornung's occasional disdain for rules might have struck a reluctantly responsive chord in the rebel that was buried under layers of discipline in the coach's personality, reminding him of those days as banker of the Fordham dormitory crap game or the times when he sneaked out of the hall in defiance of the curfew.

When it came to rules for the Packers, however, Lombardi was even-handedly strict. Times had changed and he did not follow the same method of enforcement that Father Mulqueen had used when he was an undergraduate. But hitting a player with a fine hurt as much as swatting him with a broken drumstick or even a knotted light cord.

When the Packers' training camp opened at St. Norbert College, a Catholic school in De Pere, Wisconsin, Lombardi was prompt in demonstrating that the old, easygoing days were gone. Curfew was 11 P.M. Emlen Tunnell, a veteran who had played for Lombardi in New York and should have known better, lost no time in serving as an object lesson. He arrived back at 11:05 P.M. Vince was waiting at the door.

"That'll cost you fifty dollars, mister," he said, and from then on everyone started checking his watch very carefully.

Green Bay is part of the Central Time Zone, but the players soon learned they were operating on Lombardi time. If practice was scheduled for 2 P.M., a man who arrived only five minutes before that hour was considered inexcusably laggard. To be safe, many of the players turned their watches ahead by fifteen minutes to avoid last minute arrivals.

It was part of a new philosophy of football the Packers were being taught. The coach was perfectly willing to explain his reasons:

"A man who's late for meetings or for the bus won't run his pass routes right. He'll be sloppy."

Merely getting by was no longer good enough. A man had to do better than that, even when it came to catching buses. It was one way to establish the proper pattern.

"I've got to have men who bend to me," the coach explained.

And bend they did, if they stayed with the team. It was part of the price to be paid. Much of what Lombardi believed about football was entirely of a practical nature—the fundamentals of blocking, tackling, running with the ball, practiced over and over until they became unbreakable habits that helped win games. But another side to his approach to coaching was almost mystical. His players must be extensions of a single personality—his personality. They must share his emotion toward the game, and, like him, they must try to control that emotion but not hide it.

Most of all, they must be able to excel under pressure—pressure from the opponents, pressure from their own belief in their talents, but particularly pressure from the volatile man from Brooklyn who had waited all his life for a chance like this and was going to do whatever was necessary to make sure that the wait had not been in vain.

Chapter 10

The Lombardi School of Applied Psychology

At the Packers' first training camp under Vince Lombardi, the rookies were required to report three days early. Several veterans also showed up before the full squad was required to report. One of them was Max McGee. A difference of opinion soon arose between McGee and the coach on whether the evening curfew and other such rules applied to the players who had reported before they'd been scheduled to arrive.

If a man was in training camp, Lombardi said, he was subject to the same restrictions as the rookies. McGee couldn't see it that way. He left and did not return until the three-day preliminary session was over. Lombardi met him in a hallway. He lunged for Max, grabbed him, and started to bang his head against the wall, yelling until the window panes rattled.

McGee wasn't hurt physically, but his feelings were bruised.

"I'm not going to play for this thus-and-so," he said, approximately. "He's a madman."

McGee was still boiling mad an hour later when he met the coach on the way to a meeting of the squad. Lombardi slapped him on the back.

"Come on, Max," he said. "Let's get to the meeting."

It seemed to McGee as they walked along amiably together that Vince had completely forgotten the incident in the hallway. Perhaps he had. As the training session wore on, it became obvious to the Lombardi-watchers that while he sometimes had an alarmingly short fuse, his anger passed as quickly as it came and a few minutes later he'd forgotten what he'd been so sore about.

Some of the more perceptive Lombardi-watchers became convinced that part of the time, at least, the coach's explosions were calculated rather than spontaneous. According to the Lombardi one-man school of applied psychology, a winning coach must be able to get inside his players' psyches and motivate them. One of those who was a special target of the coach's sometimes devious methods of motivation-tinkering was a large and talented young man from Idaho named Jerry Kramer.

"You look like an old cow," the coach kept yelling at him. "You run like an old cow. Kramer, you're the worst guard I've ever seen."

No one had ever talked to Jerry that way before. Other coaches had yelled at him now and then, of course, but in general he'd always been told that he was a pretty fine sort of fellow with great potential. Under the coach's goading, he lost seven pounds in a single practice session as he tried to work hard enough to satisfy that gadfly on the sidelines who kept downgrading his talents. He finished practice at last and dragged wearily to the locker room. He took off his helmet and sat on a bench with his head down, wondering why he'd ever left Idaho—wondering, too, how he'd ever been deluded into thinking that he could play football for the pros.

Lombardi sensed that Jerry had been pushed just far enough. He walked over to him and reached out and mussed his hair.

"Son," he said, "one of these days you're going to be the greatest guard in the league."

Kramer was one of the players in whom Lombardi saw enough potential to be worth yelling at, cajoling, threatening, praising, or whatever else it took to make them more close to the goal of perfection he sought for them. In Jerry's case, the fact that he played Vince's old position, the one he'd played for Fordham, may have had a bearing on the matter. But he was only one of those on the squad who were talented enough that the coach sought to force them or con them or even trick them into playing up to their innate capacities.

Apparently on the theory that the first-year men were already scared enough, Lombardi seldom yelled at them. He sought excuses to single them out for praise. He studied their personalities. During the 1959 training season, he decided that one rookie was potentially useful but handicapped by shyness. He issued his orders. From then on, the young man never had a chance to feel lonely.

When he climbed aboard the team bus, one of the veterans hurried over to share his seat. On the plane, at the dinner table, on the sidelines, one of the respected old-timers was constantly at his elbow, being friendly.

The rookie couldn't understand why he'd suddenly become so socially acceptable, but he was delighted by his new-found popularity. His personality blossomed under the treatment. His team spirit was a joy to behold. Most important, his football improved and one more victory could be chalked up to the Lombardi theories of applied psychology.

The next year, when the youth was a second-year man, Lombardi started yelling at him, criticizing him, pointing out defects at the top of his voice. But by then, the former rookie was well enough established to be able to survive phase two of the Lombardi method and even profit by some of the advice.

During the 1959 training season, Lombardi reached some conclusions about which players would fit into his theory of football playing and which would not. Among those who were found wanting was Bill Howton, who had been something of a star with the Packers before Vince's arrival, if a team that can't beat anyone but Philadelphia can be said to have stars. Howton had scored forty-three touchdowns since he joined Green Bay in 1952, and Lombardi was willing to admit he was a good player. But he was not his kind of player, so he had to go.

Howton was traded, along with a number of other players who had supposed their futures with the Packers were secure. In return, Lombardi acquired some men in whom he detected potentials that had been overlooked elsewhere.

Fred Thurston was one. Fuzzy had been a journeyman lineman who had not found a permanent home in Philadelphia, Chicago, or Baltimore, but Lombardi felt he would be an asset to the Packers and sure enough, he was. Others were Henry Jordan, who had been a second-string tackle with the Browns, and Bill Quinlan, who had been idle in Cleveland during the 1958 season because of a broken leg. Emlen Tunnell, whose distinguished career with the Giants seemed to be about over, was added to leaven the Packers' line with experience. Tunnell had played for New York while his new boss was still an assistant coach at Fordham, but the coach felt he had another good season or two left in him.

The Packers' reputation as one of the worst teams in the league helped during the trading season. If another team had a player who was considered expendable but who might turn out to be a star, it was better to send him to a perennial also-ran like Green Bay than to take a chance trading him to a contender. And so Lombardi wheeled and dealed and acquired reinforcements, including a new quarterback, McHan. The coach liked

Starr, who worked hard and paid attention and obeyed the rules. Bart was intelligent enough to be a quarterback, no doubt about that. But Lombardi wondered if he was not too gentlemanly for this game, too lacking in self-confidence. He kept him around, but he did not yet consider him first string.

In his attempts to improve the squad before the season began, Lombardi was in no position to bolster the trading potential by sweetening the offer with cash. As coach, he would have been willing to spend whatever was necessary to produce a winner. But as general manager, he knew Green Bay couldn't afford it. In 1958, the Packers had made a net profit of only $37,300 on a gross of $836,000. In most cities, a coach might go to the owner and ask him to dig into his pocket for some additional financing, but not in Green Bay. The Packers were owned by a nonprofit organization, the stock held by numerous residents who had come forward and chipped in to keep the club solvent. They were forbidden to collect dividends on their investments, but the owners were not likely to throw any more money in the pot for buying a more talented group of players.

By consulting with General Manager Lombardi, Coach Lombardi could see plainly enough that the road toward a less shaky financial underpinning for the club lay in the direction of producing a winning team. If he could come up with an improved win-loss record, the other problems would solve themselves. And so Vince went about acquiring talent where he could, most of the trades turning out to be shrewd ones. But he made a few mistakes, notably in the case of a rookie from Ball State named Tim Brown.

Brown was fast and carried the ball well. But Hornung and Taylor were available, the club had three other talented backs, and when Brown dropped a punt during the season's opening game with the Chicago Bears the coach decided Tim was not worth keeping. He banished him to Philadelphia, where he proceeded to set league records for most yards gained in a game and in a season.

Despite the trades, all but a dozen of the players who represented Green Bay in the fall of '59 were survivors of the squad that had established the worst record in Packers history the year before. Most of them had been recruited by Liz Blackbourn, the rest by Scooter McLean. They had become accustomed to being losers. They had not learned to like it, but they had learned to live with the reputation of a team that nearly always came in on the short end of the score. Lombardi had used his voice, his psychology, and his teaching methods to try to make winners of them. But before they could acquire the properly confident attitude he sought, it was necessary that they learn how it felt to win.

That meant that the exhibition season was important. The games would not count in the standings, but the coach approached them with a kind of controlled ferocity that ended any lingering doubts that life had changed for the survivors from the 1958 squad.

Lombardi did not keep his coaching creed a secret. It could be summed up in six words, he said: "To win, to win, to win."

Some of the newspapermen who watched the Packers prepare for the exhibition games went away to commune with their typewriters and try to describe the coach. One wrote, for example, that "compared to Vince, Simon Legree was a gentle humanitarian." The visitors tended to find Lombardi more interesting than his players, and the result was the first trickle of what was to become a sweeping torrent, a flood of words in newspapers, magazines, and finally in books about the man who was rebuilding a team in his own image. Not all the words were complimentary, by any means, and Vincent resented some of them. But even the critical remarks helped put him on the road to becoming the best known professional football coach of all time.

Not many of the men who came to watch Lombardi at work understood his methods as yet, but some of them learned in the years to come. As the exhibition season of 1959 approached, there was considerable interest beyond Wisconsin's boundaries in whether the methods would work. The test, as the coach was the first to point out, was whether the team won.

And it did win. The Packers took four of the six exhibition games, changing the habits of recent years. Then the team not only won its opener from the Bears but, a week later, upset the Detroit Lions 28 to 10, then took the San Francisco Forty-Niners 21 to 20.

After the 9 to 6 victory over Chicago, Lombardi had said his defensive team played well, but he was disappointed in the offense—it had tended to get too emotional, said this man of emotion. It was hard to complain about the early season record of 3-0, however, which put the Packers in first place in the league's Western Division. Coach Lombardi was pleased and so was General Manager Lombardi. All three games had been played in Green Bay and all three had been sellouts, with the stadium's 32,150 seats filled for the first time in years. The Packer fans were talking championship, and Lombardi gave the team's press agent an unusual assignment—dampening their enthusiasm. Tom Miller, the public relations man, went on radio and television to pass along the message: "Don't raise your hopes—this can't continue indefinitely."

The next game was with the Los Angeles Rams and was played in Milwaukee. The Rams scrambled and struggled for a lead, going ahead 2 to 0 on a safety, then adding a field goal to make it 5 to 0 and a touchdown to lead 11 to 0 before the Packers managed a field goal in return. Each team made another field goal to put the score at 14 to 6. But then the Packers' defense, which had been carrying the burden, fell apart and when the game was over the Rams had won 45 to 6.

A fluke, the Packer backers said. But no, the Baltimore Colts took the next game 45 to 21, and when Green Bay headed east to play the Giants their season record was 3-2.

Lombardi wanted this one. He wanted to win them all, but he had special reasons for hoping to whip the Giants. They were from his hometown, and his eastern friends had been saying that he was foolish for having gone to Green Bay, the Siberia of the NFL. Winning this game would prove something.

As it turned out, it proved only that New York had a better team. The score was 20 to 3, and the Packers had evened their season record by losing three straight.

Unlike some of the team's followers, the coach had not expected to win the title, but at the very least he wanted his team to win more than it lost. But now a new problem arose. McHan was injured. That left it up to a second-string quarterback named Bart Starr, who hadn't won a game in three years of trying.

Chicago was next. The Packers had won from the Bears, so perhaps they could do it again. But they lost and then it was the Colts' turn to beat them. That meant they had lost five of eight games, and the only encouraging sign was that the offensive team had proved it could score points under its new leader. Starr and the others had made forty-one points in the Chicago and Baltimore games, which hadn't been enough to win but was an indication that Lombardi might have erred in keeping Bart on the bench. The coach had more confidence in him now. More important, Starr had confidence in himself.

On a forward pass play, Lombardi pointed out, the quarterback was entitled to exactly 3.5 seconds to get the ball away. It was up to the line to give him those 3.5 seconds. It all sounded very simple, talking about it at the locker room bull sessions, but of course it was not nearly as simple on the field. One more defeat in the last four games and the best the Packers could hope for would be a .500 season. That was more than almost anyone had expected, including Lombardi, before the season began, but it would mean that the chance for a winning year would be gone. The coach had kept saying he had never been associated with a loser and wasn't planning to start now, but it seemed likely that he'd have to get accustomed to the idea.

Washington was next, then Detroit. With Taylor and Hornung carrying the ball and with Starr fading back and standing in the eye of the storm while the action swirled around him, then getting the pass away before the 3.5 seconds of grace was quite over, Green Bay won both these games and was back to even, five games won, five lost. Los Angeles was next and the memory of that 45 to 6 defeat loomed large.

But the machine that Lombardi had fashioned was beginning to function, and the team that traveled to the West Coast to meet the Rams was not like the one that had spent such a frustrating afternoon in Milwaukee's County Stadium five Sundays earlier. This time the Packers won 38 to 20 and stayed in California to take the season's final game from San Francisco. That made the season's record 7-5, good enough for third place and the best percentage for Green Bay since 1944.

And so it was all over for 1959 except the balloting for "coach of the year." Jim Lee Howell, whose Giants had won the Eastern Division, got four of the sportswriters' votes in the annual Associated Press poll. Weeb Ewbank, whose Colts had won the Western Division, got two. Red Hickey of San Francisco got two.

The other twenty-nine votes went to Lombardi, a man whose only previous head coaching experience had been with St. Cecelia's High School. It was an unusual honor for a rookie, even a rookie who had passed his forty-sixth birthday.

The honor was not an unmixed blessing, however. It put its holder on the spot. Improving on the 1958 team's record had been one thing. Improving on the 1959 finish would be more difficult. Besides, as Vince had kept explaining to his players, more is expected of a second-year man, and the standards for judging him are different from those that apply to a rookie. The first season in Green Bay was over, but the pressure was building.

Chapter 11

Division Championship— Not Good Enough

In December of 1959, Lombardi attended the league meeting in New York to draw up schedules for the following fall. His old Fordham classmate, Wellington Mara, was there, and it was natural that Vince and the Giants' owner would get together for a chat. Reporters saw them and jumped to the conclusion that Vince was going to move back to New York and replace Jim Lee Howell. It was known that the Giants' coach was thinking about moving into the front office, relinquishing his place on the sidelines, and what would be more natural than that his former assistant would return to replace him?

Lombardi issued denials. The Packers' executive committee said there was nothing to it. The Giants made the denials unanimous. It was some time later when Jack Mara, the New York club's president, admitted that Vince had been offered the job. Furthermore, he hadn't said no.

There had been a quiet understanding between the Maras and Lombardi before he left New York that he would have first crack at Howell's job when it became vacant. By late in the 1959 season, Jim Lee had told his bosses that one more year would be enough. Wellington Mara told Lombardi how things stood, but it was agreed that a decision would be postponed until after the 1960 season. There was that five-year contract with Green Bay to consider, but it is hard to hold a coach who would prefer to go elsewhere, and the insiders who knew the details of the conversation between Mara and Lombardi would have been willing to give odds that Jim Lee's successor would come from Green Bay.

Meanwhile, another season approached, and when training camp convened it was the mixture as before. There were the grass drills, the wind sprints, the building up of pressures to perform. As Lionel Aldridge was to explain the Lombardi philosophy some years later, players learned that "you either fit yourself to the mold or you don't, and if you don't you get a free ride to the airport."

While wearing his general manager's hat, Lombardi could see statistical evidence of the difference a winning record had made. The applications for season tickets in Green Bay increased from 25,000 to 31,000, almost enough to fill the stadium for each home game without worrying about single-ticket sales. The time had not yet arrived when a fan had to inherit the right to buy a season ticket, an asset he valued more than gold or diamonds, but it was rapidly approaching.

"I'm here because we win," the coach reminded his players as the season opener approached. "You're only here because we win. When we lose, we're gone."

Once again, the exhibition games were prepared for with almost as much determination as if they counted in the standings and this time the Packers took all six of them. But the momentum was broken when they lost to the Bears in the opener. Mistakes were made, but Lombardi said that the value of mistakes was to learn from them and then forget them.

Perhaps the team did learn, because it won the next four games. The fans began to say that at last the Pack was going to win another championship, after sixteen years of trying. Lombardi did not say so, however.

Baltimore won, with Johnny Unitas picking apart the Green Bay defenses. The Packers beat Dallas and nearly won from the Rams, losing only in the final minutes in a game played in Milwaukee. A Thanksgiving Day game with Detroit was next, and with only three days to prepare for the Lions and to forget the previous Sunday's disappointing result the team couldn't meet the challenge.

"Football is a game of reactions," Lombardi said in describing what happened that afternoon in Detroit. "If you're not ready emotionally, you can't react properly. You will get beat by a step or by inches. We were ready physically but not mentally or emotionally, and we played our worst game and got beat."

If a team was not up for a game, a considerable share of the blame must go to the coach, Lombardi believed. One of a coach's functions was the care and feeding of the diverse psychological hangups that affect players' skills. During the week that followed the loss to the Lions, Vince paid close attention to the psyches of the young men in his charge, a process that was not pleasant for anyone concerned but showed results. The Chicago Bears were the first to discover that the Packers were no longer the inept crew that had looked so frustrated in losing to the Lions. After a nine day interval between the Thanksgiving disaster and the rematch with Chicago, an interval spent listening to the sound of the coach's voice, the Green Bay representatives were ready to uphold the truth of one of the football cliches in which Lombardi believed: "They came to play."

The Packers came on the field with a sense of relief at finally being released from the Lombardi pressure cooker in which they'd been stewing since leaving Detroit. The Bears had won the opener but this time they lost. The score was 41 to 13, an indication of how determined the Green Bay players were that they would not undergo another week like the last one.

The momentum built up during the aftermath of the poor showing in Detroit carried the Packers to victories in the season's last two games, giving them an 8-4 record. That was only slightly better than in 1959 but it was good enough to make them champions of the Western Division, qualifying them to play the Eastern Division's representative, the Philadelphia Eagles.

The Philadelphia Eagles? Yes. While Lombardi had been dragging the Packers out of the swampy ground in which they'd been mired for so long, a renaissance had also taken place in Philadelphia. Buck Shaw took the job that Vince had turned down there, and the Eagles had climbed from last place to first in their division, winning two games more in 1960 than Green Bay did.

The playoff was held in Franklin Field the day after Christmas, with the National Broadcasting Company paying $200,000 for the right to televise it. Paul Hornung, who had been the league's high scorer during the season with 176 points, kicked off. Tim Brown, who had been cut from the Packers because he'd dropped a punt, handled the return and the game was on.

The first break of the game went against Philadelphia as Bill Quinlan intercepted Norm Van Brocklin's pass. The Packers moved down to the Eagles' six-yard line, two yards away from a first down.

In retrospect, Lombardi decided that the next play was the turning point of the game. It was part of his philosophy that a team that gets that close to the goal line must not come away empty-handed. It was fourth down. A field goal would put Green Bay ahead, but for once the coach decided to gamble. Instead of sending in his kicking unit, he ordered Bart Starr to give the ball to Jim Taylor.

The linemen did what they were supposed to do. They opened a momentary hole large enough for the fullback to move ahead for a first down. But Taylor's foot slipped. The hole closed. It was Philadelphia's ball on the five-yard line and the score was still 0-0.

Late in the game, the Eagles led 17 to 13. The Packers moved the ball from their thirty-five to Philadelphia's thirty. With twenty-five seconds left, those lost three points in the first quarter took on new significance. If the score was 17 to 16, as it might have been, a field goal would now be enough to win. As it was, nothing but a touchdown would do, and once more Starr handed the ball to Taylor and the line opened a hole for him.

For a moment, it looked as if he was going to score. He plunged through the opening, crossed the twenty, the fifteen, the ten, and the crowd was on its feet yelling. But when the goal was only nine yards away, the Eagles had him. He was wrestled to the ground and, for all practical purposes, the season was over.

Afterward, Lombardi could have blamed Hornung, who had missed a thirteen-yard field goal late in the first half. He could have mentioned Max McGee's thirty-yard punt, which gave the Eagles a chance for their first touchdown. Instead, he blamed himself.

"I made the wrong guess," he said.

Despite the defeat in the playoff game, however, Green Bay's two successful seasons under Lombardi had made him a celebrity. Reporters and the coach did not always get along, but they found him interesting and eminently quotable. Another factor was the increased role of television. Audiences for the games were growing to the point where many Americans regularly spent their Sunday afternoons crouched before a TV set during the football season. Green Bay might be the smallest city in the league and hardly comparable to New York or Chicago in most ways, but its team had proved it could whip the big cities' boys and its coach found himself in the national spotlight.

He had waited a long time to fulfill his wife's prediction that he would be a second Knute Rockne, but now less biased sources were implying the same thing. When a national magazine told its readers that Lombardi "seems certain to become one of the greatest coaches of all time," it made pleasant reading.

Vince had mixed feelings about his sudden fame, however. The publicity heated up the pressure, not only on him but on his team. It seemed that he would have to keep winning or be branded a failure, and even winning brought some new hazards.

"The other teams will be ready for us," he pointed out. "Everybody wants to knock off the [divisional] champion. Then, too, there is a tendency to get fatheaded—players and coaches alike. The ego takes over and you are no longer willing to pay the price."

He made it clear that anyone who expected to coast through the 1961 season on the strength of his press clippings would be disappointed. Winning the division championship did not mean he would hesitate to get rid of any of them who failed to produce.

"Football is a hardheaded, cold business," he said. "No matter what a player did last year, if he can't do it this year, he has got to go."

The players could relax between the playoff and the start of the training season, but the combination coach and general manager would have no time off. Lombardi said that was fine with him. If it weren't for his responsibilities as general manager, he told friends that winter of 1960, he would be unhappy.

"I thrive on work. I'm restless, worrisome, demanding, sometimes impatient and hot tempered. For those characteristics, a full schedule is the best antidote."

He did not say so in public, but another problem was hanging over his head—whether to leave Green Bay and take over the Giants. He had left the door open to the change when the Maras had suggested it a year before, but now the situation was different.

For one thing, the Packers were now a better team than the Giants, as indicated by the 1960 standings. More important, professional football was rapidly changing. The American Football League was raiding NFL rosters, and club owners were becoming very sensitive about contract jumping. If Vince left Green Bay with three years to go on the agreement he'd signed, it would weaken the league's case. If he chose to return triumphantly to his hometown as coach of the Giants, he could probably find a way to do so despite the contract, but he decided against it.

If there were regrets, Lombardi kept them to himself. He plunged into preparations for the new season. The schedule was to be longer— fourteen games to play, instead of twelve. The team roster would be limited to thirty-six men, which was cutting things somewhat thin.

"The team with the fewest injuries will win the title," Vince predicted.

There was another worry. Hornung and several other established players might have to leave for military service. Hornung's loss would be a serious blow—"Paul is really a very ordinary halfback until he gets fifteen yards from the goal," Lombardi said. "Then he's the greatest. You see, he can't do anything but score points."

Hornung had broken the league's point-scoring record set in 1942 by another Green Bay star, Don Hutson. But when he was asked to explain the resurgence of the Packers he said Lombardi deserved the credit.

"Lombardi raises hell," he added, which seemed like explanation enough.

As always, the coach was looking for rookies to reinforce the ranks, and one of those he wanted was a star backfield man at Michigan State, Herb Adderley. The Canadian League also wanted him. Lombardi sent one of his assistants, Bill Austin, to sign him up.

The Canadian representative arrived simultaneously, and an argument developed in a parking lot, climaxed by Austin and the other league's representative trading punches while Adderley looked on in astonishment. When the fracas ended, Herb put the Packer contract on the hood of one of the cars and signed it.

Before long, he had second thoughts. The first weeks of training camp meant nothing but frustration. He had been an offensive back in college, but Lombardi told him he was now a flanker. He had good speed. He could catch passes. He looked great in practice. But when he got in a game he looked terrible.

Lombardi praised him when he did something right, yelled at him when he did something wrong, and, in between, tried to reason with him like a stern but loving father. Nothing worked. Finally, with the frustration building up in both the coach and Adderley, Lombardi asked Emlen Tunnell to do a little detective work. Having years of experience with the locker room grapevine, he was assigned to learn why the rookie wasn't living up to his promise. Emlen sloped off to find out and was soon back with the word:

"He doesn't want to be a flanker. He wants to be a defensive back."

Why not? He certainly wasn't cutting it as a flanker The coach switched Adderley's assignment, a decision he did not regret. Herb went on to become an all-pro on the Packers' defensive team and an object lesson for Lombardi, who freely admitted he'd made a mistake.

"He is a natural defensive back and that's where he's going to play," Lombardi announced.

As training camp came to a close and Green Bay headed toward a defense of its Western Division title, the Packers no longer fielded a team whose members were little known outside of Wisconsin. It seemed to be true, as one national sportswriter said, that they had "no great passer, no great receiver, no breakaway back—the standard prerequisites for a successful pro team." But that didn't seem to matter because, as the New York critic went on, Green Bay "uses rugged, old-fashioned blocking to open holes for rugged, old-fashioned ball carriers."

Lombardi considered Taylor, Hornung, and Tom Moore "the three finest running backs in the league as a group—maybe one individual here and there has an edge, but no other team has a group as good as ours."

Chapter 12

The Rise of the Packer Dynasty

During the 1961 season, more than four million persons paid to watch NFL teams play, and, for the first time since the league was organized, tickets were hard to get in nearly every stadium. In Milwaukee, where many seats had been empty before Lombardi's era at Green Bay, the Packers drew an average of 45,145 to a stadium with an official capacity of 44,450. At Green Bay, you couldn't have squeezed another fan into the stadium with a shoehorn. This was the year when Lombardi's team was expected to win and it did. But there were complications.

One was Hawg Hanner's appendix. When the defensive tackle's doctor insisted he couldn't wait until the end of the season to have it out, he was reluctantly excused from the next game. But on the following Sunday, only ten days after his operation, Hanner was back in the line. He was hurting but, as Lombardi's father had told him long ago, hurt is in the mind.

As Jerry Kramer once pointed out, the coach had the highest threshold of pain in the world—"None of our injuries hurts him at all." But even Lombardi had to admit Kramer had a valid excuse for leaving the lineup midway in the season when he broke his leg. He said later that, when Jerry went to the hospital, "I doubted very much that we could stay in the race." Kramer was the league's outstanding guard, his coach said, perhaps the best guard in the history of the game, a 240-pounder who could "run with any back we had."

In addition, Hornung, Boyd Dowler, and Ray Nitschke were called up by the Army. The military was willing to let them join the team on weekends and they did, but having three of the regulars miss all the practice sessions did not ease the coach's burdens.

But, in Lombardi's words, the Packers "were a dedicated team which met great adversity." Despite his part-time status, Hornung played well enough to be voted the league's outstanding player. Improvising and making changes to meet each new crisis, the Packers struggled through the season to win eleven of the fourteen games, a record that gave them the Western Division title for the second year in a row. The honor carried with it the right to meet the Giants for the championship.

Green Bay, in the old days under Lambeau, had won six league championships, but the 1961 game was the first title game to be played in the Packers' home stadium. Banners went up bragging that this was "Titletown, USA." The weatherman did his bit for the local heroes by arranging for several days of subzero cold, setting a tradition for future playoffs and giving the New York visitors new evidence for the old claim that this was the Siberia of the league.

The Army cooperated by letting its three most publicized members, Hornung, Nitschke, and Dowler, return for the war with New York. The Giants' forces were led by a crafty quarterback named Y. A. Tittle and brought with them a reputation as the nation's best defensive team. The game looked like an even match, with Tittle's passing likely to spell the difference.

But Lombardi had waited a long time to show his hometown what he'd been doing out here in the provinces, and his players made sure there was no repetition of 1960's disappointment in Philadelphia. The final score was 37 to 0 in Green Bay's favor, and the game was as one-sided as those figures indicate.

Bart Starr, who'd been considered no better than a journeyman quarterback by the eastern publicity mills, passed for three touchdowns. Tittle, who'd been given the special treatment reserved for a star who's lucky enough to be playing for New York, had a horrible afternoon, with four of his passes intercepted. Hornung scored nineteen points. All in all, it was a most convincing demonstration that Lombardi and the rough young men who worked for him had put together a football machine that was the best in the land.

The Green Bay fans, who had learned in years of adversity to be philosophical about losing, saw their duty plainly. If the Packers could win the league championship, it was up to them to celebrate by tearing down the goal posts. That the goal posts were made of steel didn't matter.

Down they went, to be sawed up into chunks and enshrined on mantel-pieces along the Fox River Valley forever.

The players had learned by now what to expect from their coach. According to his unwritten textbook on clinical psychology, a defeat called for a temporary easing of the pressure to make sure it would be forgotten so it would not happen again. A victory, on the other hand, must be followed by the kind of criticism that is good for a football man's soul—and for his head, which must not be allowed to get too large for the helmet.

But how can you criticize a 37-0 victory that brought Green Bay an NFL title? Lombardi found a way.

He admitted they had played pretty well—not perfectly, of course, but not at all bad. But that only meant they had more to live up to in the future.

"Now you're going to find out what kind of men you are," he told his players. "It takes a lot more of a man to perform as a champion than it did to get him there."

Listening to the coach, they had no trouble understanding what his words meant: more grass drills, more wind sprints, more shouts of criticism from the sidelines. It might be the last day of December, the season over, the championship won. But next July's training camp torture was already looming ahead.

Green Bay had won the league title only three years after the team had posted the worst record in its history. It was up to Lombardi to make sure the hazards of winning, like the hazards of losing, were surmounted.

Fourteen of the twenty-two starting players who reported in the summer of 1962 were holdovers from 1958. Several of the other starters were also veterans, picked up in trades. But when practice began, the coach started explaining football as if they were newcomers to the game.

The Green Bay power sweep, for example, was familiar even to the casual bystanders by now, but the coach ran off his films of the play—it was designated either as 49 or 28, depending on which direction it went—as if he'd just invented it.

The veterans understood and the rookies soon learned that part of the price to be paid for winning under Lombardi was to be able to sit quietly under a tongue lashing, remembering only to murmur, "Yes, sir," when it was over. They had discovered that orders were meant to be obeyed and at once—as Henry Jordan said, "When he tells me to sit down, I don't even look for a chair."

Jordan was a man with considerable talent and a wry sense of humor, but sometimes he got tired of hearing his boss yell at him.

"Why do you chew me out all the time instead of this other guy?" he demanded once.

Lombardi had an explanation.

"I'm chewing you out because he needs it," he told Jordan. "He's not the kind who can take this kind of chewing out."

The players were professionals, playing for money, but they found themselves unable to take a neutral attitude toward their coach. Sometimes they hated him, sometimes they regarded him with unmixed affection, and the emotions could occur in the same man's mind within a matter of minutes.

He was a tough fellow, coaching a team that was also tough, but he could be a softy, too.

One time, after the victory over the Giants in the 1961 playoff, three hundred of his old friends and relatives gave him a welcome home party in Sheepshead Bay. His eyes turned misty early in the evening. Another day he attended the ordination of a priest, Guy McPartland, who had played for him at St. Cecelia's. He wept openly and unashamedly.

His laugh was as uninhibited as his voice—you could hear it across the noise of a crowded room. He passed the basic test of a sense of humor by being able to appreciate a joke on himself. He had his share of ego, no doubt of that, but the honors that began to come his way he found amusing as well as pleasant. When an ethnic club voted him "Italian of the Year," he inquired, "Where does that leave Pope John?"

When the momentary anger passed, he could joke with players who sometimes bent the rules he had laid down. He liked to tell of how he had fined Max McGee $250 for breaking curfew one night and, a few nights later, fined him $500 for breaking it again.

"The next time it will be $1,000," he said, then added, "If you find anything worth $1,000, let me know—I may go with you."

Some of his players were now famous wherever football was known. Their names were worth large sums in testimonials. Business opportunities were coming their way. But Lombardi continued to treat them like students of the game—and not very bright students, at that.

"Talent is not only a blessing, it is a burden—as the gifted ones will soon find out," he warned.

His wife, Marie, said she sometimes felt sorry for a boy whose natural gifts made Lombardi feel he could become an outstanding player.

"Vin will just open a hole in that boy's head and pour everything he knows into it, and there's no way out of it," she said. "I don't want to watch it."

As always, Lombardi was seeking nothing less than perfection, although he recognized that it was not attainable in an imperfect world.

"You will make mistakes," he told his players after one practice session. "But not very many, if you want to play for the Green Bay Packers."

The 1962 team breezed through its exhibition season unbeaten and began to win in the early season with monotonous regularity, whipping Minnesota, St. Louis, and Chicago in succession. Winning was always the goal, but the players found compliments were hard to come by, at least from the coach.

"I don't want to seem ungrateful," he told them. "I'm awfully proud of you guys, really. You've done a hell of a job. But sometimes you just disgust me."

Now that he was a winner, Lombardi discovered he had a lot of potential new friends. He reacted by limiting his social circle. Some people in Green Bay and elsewhere criticized him for this, but most of those with whom he felt comfortable were men he'd known in the days before he was being hailed as a football genius.

His players also were subject to the temptations associated with the easy popularity that comes to a winner. He worried about them—some of them more than others. He laid down strict rules. No standing at a bar, even if the drink was ginger ale. Neckties to be worn in the hotel dining room even if the hour was 7 A.M. They were in the public eye; they must behave accordingly.

One afternoon, looking out the window of the East Side hotel where he was staying in Milwaukee, he saw two of his players walking past with a pair of businessmen who were known to bet on the games. They were on their way to a restaurant where other bettors hung out.

"That will be the end of that," Lombardi told his companion.

It was. Neither those two players nor any other members of the team ever again entered the doors of the controversial restaurant.

As the 1962 season moved ahead, such words as "machine" and "dynasty" were being used to describe the Packers. Since the middle of the 1959 season, changes had been rare in Lombardi's starting lineup. Only Willie Wood, Ron Kramer, Willie Davis, Ray Nitschke, and Herb Adderley had managed to join the top twenty-two men on the offensive and defensive squads. The defense was particularly strong. It allowed only seven points in the first three games of the season. In the fourth game, Detroit equaled that total and with two minutes to go it seemed that the seven points would be enough.

But with the Packers trailing 7 to 6, Adderley intercepted a pass, Hornung kicked a field goal, and Green Bay stayed undefeated.

In the season's second game with Minnesota, Hornung was hurt but Tom Moore took his place, and when the Packers went to Detroit on Thanksgiving Green Bay had a 10-0 record. The Lions were in second place in the division and Lombardi had prepared his game plan carefully. The trouble was that Detroit failed to follow the script.

It was this game that stuck in Lombardi's memory after the season was over. He cited it as an example of what can happen when a team is prepared for one kind of tactics and fails to adapt quickly enough to another. The Lions changed their style of defensive play so successfully that in the first half they dropped Bart Starr eight times, the losses adding up to seventy-six yards. Once they caught him in the end zone for a safety. Once they recovered a fumble. At halftime the Packers were behind 23 to 0.

Things changed in the second half. Detroit was held to one field goal in the final two quarters and the Packers scored two touchdowns. But the adjustment had come too late. Lombardi gave a characteristic explanation of the only loss of the year. It was caused, he said, by "coaching stupidity."

In the history of the league, no team had ever won more than thirteen games in a regular season, and Green Bay's 13-1 record was the best since Chicago went undefeated in a thirteen-game season in 1934, the year Vince enrolled as a Fordham freshman. Some years later, Lombardi said that the 1962 team was his greatest and he had the statistics to prove it. In the rating system he used, that team ranked first in both offense and defense when compared to the others he coached. During the year, it scored 415 points and allowed only 148.

With three divisional championships in four years at Green Bay, Lombardi led his team to New York to try for a second consecutive league championship. The weather around Yankee Stadium was homelike—one magazine writer claimed "it was the coldest day since Perry discovered the North Pole," but he was not from Green Bay.

When the Packers arrived in New York, Lombardi checked into the Manhattan Hotel. He and his wife were sitting in their suite, chatting with a Chicago newspaperman, when the telephone rang. Vince picked it up.

"No, no, I'm too busy," he said. "I tell you it's out of the question. Forget it."

It had been the league publicity man, informing him that a hundred reporters were waiting at the Americana Hotel for a press conference. Lombardi went on drinking his coffee. The phone rang again. This time it was Pete Rozelle, the league's commissioner, and for once Lombardi lost an argument. Reluctantly he put on his coat and took a cab to the Americana, where he was greeted by cheers from the waiting newsmen. Lombardi grinned and said he was ready for the questions. Dick Young of the New York *Daily News* spoke up first:

"Vinnie, you are coming back to your hometown for a championship game. Do you think there's any chance the officials might tend to be 'homers'?"

Lombardi snorted. He glared at Young as if he was a rookie who'd just fumbled a kickoff return.

"That's the silliest question I've ever heard," he said, turned on his heel, and stalked out of the room. The press conference was over.

The weather did not improve. The cold would not hurt the ticket sale—by now, football fans were willing to put up with anything—but New Yorkers were grumbling a lot. Visitors from Green Bay kept pointing out that this would be considered only a mild cold snap back home.

Even a hardy northlander would admit that the sheets of ice surrounding the playing surface were impressive, however, and the ground was as unyielding as steel. New York was out for revenge for the licking of a year before, hoping to prove that all the excitement stirred up by the Wisconsin invaders and their coach was unjustified.

The pattern was set early in the game when Jimmy Taylor had the ball. He headed directly for Sam Huff, a linebacker who played with the same controlled ferocity as the Packers' fullback. Huff drove him out of bounds and used his knees and elbows to excellent advantage as the two men skidded across the ice.

Taylor staggered to his feet and leaned over, coughing blood. He wobbled back to the formation and told Starr to give him the ball. Tucking it under his arm, he headed for Huff, who was waiting eagerly. The fullback hit him like a runaway truck, knocked him down, trampled him into the frozen turf, and continued on his way. It is said that even the New York fans cheered.

The Giants' defense proved troublesome, stopping Green Bay with a single touchdown. Hornung was still hurt, and Kramer, who had never kicked a field goal in a game until the halfback was forced to give up the assignment, was on the spot. But the three field goals he kicked that afternoon were the margin of Green Bay's 16 to 7 victory.

With two national championships in two years and a record of 24-4 over two seasons, the Packers were beginning to feel unbeatable. This was an attitude Lombardi did not want to see. A reasonable amount of confidence in their abilities was fine. So was pride in their accomplishments. But he wanted them to worry, too, as he did, and to realize that winning two in a row meant only one thing: now it was time to try for a third championship.

But meanwhile, there was time to savor the taste of victory. Henry Jordan told what it meant.

"We can hold our heads high," he said. "And our wives can go shopping."

Lombardi did some shopping, too. The year before, the general manager had decreed that each of the players' wives should be given a mink stole. Now they were given their choice of a color television set or a stereo console. They also had a chance to spend the $5,888.57 each Packer got for beating New York.

The coach understood that many of the wives had survived a different era around Green Bay, as demonstrated by a story he told about the young daughter of his center, Jim Ringo.

It was an afternoon during the 1958 season, the year before Vince arrived, when the girl came home from school in tears. Ringo gathered her up in his muscular arms and asked her what was the matter.

"Daddy," she said, "are you a bum?"

It had been hard to answer a question like that during a year when the team had won only one game and lost ten. But in 1962, when the record was 13-1, the question would not be asked.

Bart Starr and Vince Lombardi before a College All-Star game in Chicago.

Jim Taylor goes up and over during Super Bowl I.

A classic matchup—the Chicago Bears' Dick Butkus eyes Packers' quarterback Bart Starr (1965).

Vince Lombardi's funeral at St. Patrick's Cathedral in New York City.
(All photos by Vernon J. Biever)

Chapter 13

The Over the Hill Squad

The theory of historical repetition is questionable, but in April of 1963 Lombardi must have felt as if he'd gone through all this before. The parallel between Paul Hornung's suspension and the difficulties that arose at West Point when Vince was assistant to Red Blaik reinforced the axiom that just when things are going right, something is sure to go wrong.

With Army, a 9-0 season had been followed by a cribbing scandal that cost the team all but two of its regulars and resulted in the cadets' losing all but two of their games.

At Green Bay, a 13-1 season and a second world championship were followed by the loss of only a single player. But that player had scored more points than anyone else in the league for three of the previous four seasons. Besides running with the ball with abandon, Hornung was useful for his blocking, his field goal kicking, and his leadership. His suspension, nearly six months before the season began, meant that winning a third straight title would be much more difficult.

The announcement of Hornung's indefinite suspension from professional football came on April 17, 1963. Commissioner Rozelle said that during the 1959, 1960, and 1961 seasons, the halfback had placed bets on NFL and college games, none of them over $500, and had "transmitted specific information concerning NFL games for betting purposes." The memory of seeing Hornung and another Packer walking along an East Side street toward the restaurant where bettors hung out must have crossed his coach's mind.

Hornung had not bet against the Packers, and no one suggested that his betting had influenced his play. But Rozelle said there would be no further review of his violation of league rules until 1964, which meant he was out for the entire 1963 season.

Hornung was not the only football player in trouble. Alex Karras of the Lions was also suspended indefinitely for gambling. Five other Lions—John Gordy, Garry Lowe, Joe Schmidt, Wayne Walker, and Sam Williams—were fined $2,000 each but would be permitted to play. The Detroit players had each bet $50 that the Packers would beat the Giants in the 1962 playoff. They had won their bets, but Rozelle had now wiped out their profits.

Hornung was contrite and Lombardi did not add to his troubles by pointing out how disappointed he was in him. All he could hope now was that Paul would be smart enough to take his suspension gracefully so he would be allowed to return to the team. A season's layoff at a time when Hornung was at the height of his career would not only lose him a year's playing time but also make it difficult for him to regain his skills.

The reaction of the fans was mixed. Some felt that the backfield star had let down the team, but others felt Rozelle had been too severe. John Holzer, a Green Bay druggist who had been following the Packers since 1919, said that "his $500 bet is like a dime bet for most of us" and went sadly about with a black armband.

Lombardi did not go into mourning, but his disappointment was deep. He had looked on the talented young man as a son. He had recognized a hidden part of himself in Hornung and had tried to persuade him to temper his rebellion and high spirits with the Lombardi method of iron self-discipline. So the player's failure was, in a way, the coach's failure as well.

But there was nothing to do but prepare for a season without the team's top scorer, a man who was one of the few squad members who could act as a safety valve for the pressure the coach's tactics built up.

There were other problems in seeking a third straight title. This team was no longer hungry, desperate to prove itself. With success came the danger of letting down. One way to counter this, Lombardi knew, was to force some of the veterans to worry about keeping their jobs, and luckily he had been able to draft some promising rookies. By adding Dave Robinson, Lionel Aldridge, Dan Grimm, and Marv Fleming to the squad, he could hope that a number of the older players would have to try harder to keep such talented young men from shoving them aside.

Except for the loss of Hornung and the addition of the draft crop, the team was basically the same one that had lost only one game the previous fall. It was a remarkable football machine and it was favored to win again. But it got off to a disastrous start. When the champions of the world lost to a squad of college boys, 20 to 17, the coach found it downright humiliating.

Lombardi disliked the College All-Star game. He wished it had never been invented. But that did not mean he expected his pros to lose it. The coach had some bitter words to say to his men when two University of Wisconsin alumni, Ron VanderKelen and Pat Richter, collaborated on the winning touchdown. Fatheadedness was a malady associated with success, and the coach detected its symptoms and described them at some length.

The chastened Packers won the rest of their exhibition games, but when the season opened they lost to the Chicago Bears 10 to 3. Mrs. Lombardi watched this frustrating game from the stands with Mrs. Gene Brusky, whose husband was the team's physician. When the difficult afternoon was over, Marie noticed her companion was crying.

"But Hazel," she told Mrs. Brusky, "it isn't that important. It was just a game."

"It isn't that. It's what they were saying to you in the stands."

Football had become a game of strong emotion for fans as well as players. In an introspective moment, Lombardi had called it a game for madmen. He wanted his players to hate their opponents. But they understood that the hate was to last only until the final whistle, when it should be transferred to those scoundrels from another city who were next on the Packers' schedule.

The coach was too busy during a game to pay attention to what the opposition fans were yelling, but his wife sometimes worried that he was in physical danger from them. That was the fall when President John F. Kennedy was assassinated. The thought occurred to Marie Lombardi as the 1963 season wore on that some nut with a rifle might take aim some afternoon at another public figure, the man on the sidelines who was coach of the Green Bay Packers.

Like many other Americans, the president's death made the Lombardis wonder if the haters were taking over and the old values were falling apart. Lombardi had admired Kennedy. Not many months before, the president had urged him to go back to West Point and coach Army.

It was only a passing remark, not an official order, and Vince had been able to ignore it.

The assassination affected Lombardi by making him wary of what was going on outside the football stadiums where he spent so much of his life, but like other Americans he went ahead and did his job, namely trying to bring another championship back to the small city that claimed to be Titletown, USA. Despite difficulties, notably an injury to Starr that kept the quarterback out of action for a month, the team managed to go through the season with only two defeats. Both of the losses were to Chicago, however, and the Bears won the division title. The Packers came in second.

The coach had a word for second place. The word was "hinkydinky." Later, when Jerry Kramer combined the literary life with playing right guard, he pointed out that only Lombardi could have used such an example of outdated, grammar school slang without any of his brawny listeners snickering or smirking.

When the Playoff Bowl—"a hinkydinky game in a hinkydinky city"—was over, Lombardi was able to sit down calmly and evaluate his team. It hadn't won, he said, but he had a soft spot in his heart for an outfit that "always hung tight in spite of discouragements." There were encouraging signs. In the last few games of the year, the coach said, "I think Starr approached true greatness." Aldridge's rookie season had been surprisingly good. But Hornung had been missing and Taylor, weakened by an attack of hepatitis and hampered by injuries, had not been as effective as in 1962.

"Yet even a lesser Taylor was a great Taylor," the coach added.

The team had worked hard, he went on. It did not have to be driven.

"But it didn't seem to relish winning as much as earlier ones. It didn't play with the same abandon."

As for Hornung, there was hope that his suspension would be lifted for the 1964 season, but it was hard to tell what the year's layoff would mean to his skills.

"He's usually not a man to work by himself," the coach said. "But he's a great athlete, a great competitor, and he must understand what a year's layoff would mean. He has understood other things about his suspension so well—kept away from undesirable places and people, handled himself with the press, and declared repeatedly he wants to come back."

As had been expected, Hornung was reinstated in the spring of 1964. He talked with the coach and agreed he would have to start early to get himself back in playing shape, probably in mid-May. Lombardi suggested mid-April would be better. They compromised on mid-April.

When training camp opened, Aldridge showed up with some flab around his middle. It was Lombardi's custom to pick out one overweight member of the squad and work everybody until that victim passed out. It soon became obvious to everyone that Lionel was the man in the spotlight this year.

The drilling was unmerciful. Everyone was suffering, Aldridge more than the rest, but he was a proud young man and determined to tough it out. Ray Nitschke was near him and as the endless afternoon wore on, the veteran gave him an urgent piece of advice.

"Fall down," he panted. "Fall down, you son-of-a-bitch."

But Aldridge survived the grass drills, and the session progressed into what the players called the nutcracker drill, with Aldridge taking about every third turn. Finally, he could take no more and passed out. When he came to, Lombardi was standing over him, looking satisfied.

"Aldridge," he said, "that's all that beer you drank in the off-season."

By then, Hornung had already finished his early reconditioning. He told what it had been like:

"The first week, he had me jogging a mile each day and running up and down the steps of the stadium twice. The next week, I jogged a mile and a half, plus three trips up and down the stadium stairs."

By July, when the camp opened, the halfback was down to his 1962 playing weight of 221 pounds. But when the season began, it quickly became obvious that the layoff had handicapped one of his multiple talents. He could still run with the ball and he could still block for Taylor, but his kicking was unreliable.

Because of missed extra points, the Packers lost one-point decisions to Baltimore and Minnesota. In a rematch with the Colts, Hornung missed five field goal attempts and the Packers lost, 24-21. Lombardi hired Ben Agajanian, a talented expert on kicking, to instruct Hornung and Jerry Kramer in the art of booting a football. Agajanian left his sporting goods business in Los Angeles to fly to Green Bay, where he said Hornung's troubles might be lack of confidence.

Hornung's kicking had been fine in the season's opener with Chicago, which Green Bay won 28 to 13. He had kicked three field goals, one from fifty-two yards out, and had made the game's longest run. Perhaps he had been inspired by a run-in with the coach the night before.

Lombardi had walked into a Chicago restaurant and spotted Paul standing at the bar with his date. Vince exploded. He ran up to the halfback, yelled at him, chased him out of the building. Then he walked back to the bar and tasted the abandoned drink. It was ginger ale, but Hornung knew better than to bring this up the next day when he was fined $500.

In the first frustrating game with the Colts, Lombardi considered a mistake by Starr even more crucial than Hornung's imperfect kicking. With less than a minute to go and Green Bay behind, 21 to 20, the coach sent in a pass play. Max McGee was to run a turn-in pattern. McGee had other ideas, however. He persuaded the quarterback that a turn-out would be more effective.

Starr faded back, the cool and controlled man in the eye of the swirling hurricane, and lofted the ball toward McGee. But the man who caught it was Don Shinnick, who was employed by the Colts. The interception helped put Baltimore on the road to a first place finish and the Packers on the way to a record of 8-5-1, the team's worst since the coach's first season in Green Bay.

Lombardi worried about Starr's habit of worrying and this was certainly a mistake to worry about. But the coach decided that the play had been a valuable lesson that made Bart a better quarterback.

"When I survived it," Starr told him, "I knew I'd never let another mistake crush me again."

Before the season began, Lombardi had chosen to get along with a talented but inexperienced center, Bob Skoronski, backed up by Ken Bowman, a University of Wisconsin player who had been an eighth-round draft choice. The departure of Jim Ringo has become a favorite part of the Lombardi legend.

When a lawyer walked into the coach's office and introduced himself as the star center's representative in contract negotiations, Vince excused himself and walked out of the room. A few minutes later, he returned.

"I believe you have come to the wrong city," he told the attorney. "Mr. James Ringo is now the property of the Philadelphia Eagles."

Lombardi had signed a new five-year contract calling for more money himself before the 1964 season began—his old one had been torn up— but he felt that player demands were getting out of hand. The Ringo incident was a way of demonstrating that no one was indispensable.

Bowman rose to the opportunity given him to replace his all-pro predecessor at center, but other complications came frequently during the season. Fuzzy Thurston was injured, which meant that Forrest Gregg had to move to guard from tackle. Skoronski, who had opened the season at center, took over Gregg's old position.

Kramer's loss later in the season was particularly costly. It turned out that, among other things, the guard was being troubled by slivers that he'd carried in his body since a boyhood accident. Rumors about Jerry's condition were spreading, and a Milwaukee reporter suggested that the way to put them to rest was to have his paper's medical writer talk to Kramer's physician.

Lombardi said no.

"Tell him to ask me. I'll give him the answers."

The medical reporter ignored this advice and got the story from the doctor. When it appeared in print, the coach was furious. The next time the sportswriter who covered the team showed up in the locker room, Lombardi berated him.

"What kind of a friend of the Packers are you?" he demanded.

It was a frustrating year all around, but Lombardi continued to follow his established routine. His wife described what life was like at home:

"On Monday, Tuesday, and Wednesday, we don't talk. On Thursday, when practice tapers off, we say hello. On Friday, he is civil. On Saturday, he is downright pleasant.

"And then on Sunday, Vince feels the game is in the boys' hands. He has done all he can. Sometimes you have to poke him to keep him awake in the car, driving to the game."

The Packers' second-place finish was no consolation. The Lombardi era of excellence seemed to be waning on the banks of the Fox. Despite the disappointing 8-5-1 record in 1964, it was pointed out, it had been quite a remarkable period while it lasted. As head coach in the pro league, Lombardi had close to a .750 record, and since his arrival in 1959 Green Bay had won more games than any other NFL team.

But of course, it was said, those days were gone. Too many of the remarkable galaxy of stars he had developed were getting old. Besides, other teams had begun to copy the Lombardi methods—the conditioning, the emphasis on fundamentals. His success had carried the seeds of its own destruction.

First the Bears, then the Colts had proved that Green Bay was no better than second in its own division. No matter how well Lombardi coached—and the critics were willing to admit he was unequaled at getting the last ounce of talent out of his men—his team was obviously over the hill.

The Lombardi contention that "there is no room for second place here" sounded ironic and a little sad now. If finishing second was hinky-dinky, as he had proclaimed for all the world to hear, then what did that make the once mighty Green Bay Packers?

Chaper 14

The Five-Quarter Playoff

Jerry Kramer had undergone no less than eight abdominal operations since he left the team during the 1964 season. He had been close to death. Now he was recovering, but Lombardi felt certain he would never be able to play football again.

The coach had played right guard for Fordham, and Kramer sometimes wondered if Lombardi's constant criticism of the way he played that position might go back to a time when Vince was one of the Seven Blocks of Granite. He came to understand, however, that all the yelling, all the shouted insults were part of Lombardi's desire to make him the best right guard in the business. Before his hospitalization, the coach believed that the goal had been reached.

But now, it seemed, Kramer's career was over. Lombardi frequently said that football was a coldly businesslike game and a player whose usefulness was ended could not expect special consideration because he had once been a star. The coach did not believe that starters should be chosen on the strength of past seasons' press clippings. He was quick to cut a man who could no longer deliver, although he preferred that someone else break the news to him that he was through.

And he was convinced that Kramer was finished. He said as much in public, which brought a quick reaction from Jerry. He said he was "completely shocked" that Vince would say such a thing. His doctors had assured him his stomach wall would be in shape for the fall festivities, and he thought their medical credentials were better than those of Doc Lombardi.

Lombardi could understand why a young man wouldn't want to admit to himself that his career was over, but he remained convinced that the

Packers could not expect any help from Jerry. But he was concerned about Kramer's future. Unless he was on the roster for another season, he would lose his pension rights. The coach didn't want to do anything illegal, but he thought the rules could be bent a little for once. He consulted Commissioner Rozelle.

"He'll never be able to play," he said. "But I want to keep his pension rights alive. How can I do it?"

"Put him on the taxi squad or something," Pete said. "We'll work out some way to protect him."

Bringing Kramer to training camp was planned as an act of compassion, nothing more. But for once it turned out that Doc Lombardi's medical diagnosis was wrong. Jerry's recovery was rapid. As the season progressed, he worked his way back into the lineup, where he was most welcome. It was a year when Starr was especially glad to see that broad back in front of him when he moved back to pass.

During the first nine games, it sometimes seemed that the quarterback spent most of his Sunday afternoons under a pile of unfriendly tacklers. He was thrown for losses forty-three times during that period, an average of nearly five times a game.

Part of the problem was the necessity to improvise a starting lineup because of injuries. Neither Kramer nor Fuzzy Thurston could start the season, so the inexperienced Bowman played center, Forrest Gregg and Dan Grimm were the guards, Bob Skoronski and a second-year man, Steve Wright, the tackles. With the return of the two regular guards, Gregg was able to go back to his role as tackle. But until late in the season, the offensive line was not up to Lombardi's exacting standards.

There were other difficulties. Taylor was hurt. Hornung was ineffective and was finally benched. The ball control type of football that Lombardi favored was no longer working, and too often the quarterback found himself throwing passes from fright or in desperation, two emotions the coach disparaged.

The defense was still strong, however. The Packers staggered and fought and improvised their way to some hairbreadth victories. By December 12, when the team arrived in Baltimore, its record was nine victories and three defeats, and if it whipped the Colts it would be in first place in the Western Division.

Father Timothy Moore, Lombardi's former boss at St. Cecelia's, drove down from New Jersey to see the game. His brother, Harry, who was also a priest, came along. The Sunday of the game, not one mass but two were held for the Catholic members of the squad, with Father Harry taking the first one. Hornung overslept. He missed the early mass and he almost was too late for the second. He came hurrying into the room just in time to attend the one conducted by Father Tim.

Paul had been warming the bench but this was a crucial game for the big money, and Lombardi remembered his own contention that Hornung was a money player. When Starr led the offensive team on the field, Paul was in the halfback position.

It had been a discouraging season for him but now the old skills returned. Before the afternoon was over, Hornung had scored five touchdowns and Green Bay was in first place. Father Tim hurried into the dressing room after the game and slapped the halfback's sweaty back.

"Hey, Paul, a little religion helps, eh?"

Hornung turned to the Irishman he liked to call "my confessor."

"Tim, you're damn' right it does."

It seemed time to put up the Titletown, USA banners in Green Bay again. But it was not a season where anything could be taken for granted. The Colts were expected to lose to the Rams because Johnny Unitas was injured and a halfback was playing quarterback. But they won. The Packers were supposed to have easy going with San Francisco, but they were tied in the final sixty-seven seconds when John Brodie's pass connected. So now Green Bay and Baltimore had identical season records of 10-3-1.

That meant a playoff was necessary to decide who would represent the Western Division and play Cleveland for the league title.

Green Bay was favored. The Colts were not the same team without Unitas, and his backup man, Gary Cuozzo, had been taken out of the December 12 game with the Packers with a shoulder separation. Tom Matte, who had handled the quarterbacking job in the 20-to-17 upset of the Rams, hadn't played at that position since his days at Ohio State and even then Coach Woody Hayes had not encouraged him to pass often. Matte had taped cards with the Colts' play signals to his wrist in Los Angeles and somehow his team had won, but Matte had not gained a single yard in the air.

The Packers won the coin toss to determine where the playoff would be held. As usual, the winter weather in Green Bay was not tropical. Wisconsin was still digging out from under a ten-inch snow that had snarled Christmas traffic. The field was covered with hay until game time to discourage freezing, but the weather was not calculated to make tourists from Maryland feel at home.

As underdogs, the Colts could play with that spirit of abandon that Vince was always advocating. Without a regular quarterback, they had a built-in excuse if they lost. They demonstrated that it would be a difficult afternoon for Packer fans on the first play after Green Bay took the kickoff.

Starr surprised the Colts by calling a pass play. The ball was caught by Bill Anderson, an end who hadn't been considered good enough to play for the Washington Redskins. They had released him and he'd sat out the 1964 season. But Lombardi offered him a job, feeling he needed another man who was familiar with catching passes in view of how many walking wounded he had on his bench. Anderson had not played often, but Boyd Dowler was slowed down by ankle and shoulder injuries and so the Washington castoff was starting the most important game of the year. Now he was carrying the ball toward the Baltimore goal, but Lenny Lyles got in his way.

The Colts halfback leaped on Anderson, knocking him down. The ball bounced along the frozen turf. Don Shinnick grabbed it and took off for the Green Bay end zone, only twenty-five yards away.

Starr was among the Packers who tried in vain to stop him. The quarterback never got close enough for a tackle because big Jim Welch got in a block that sent Bart to the sidelines with painfully bruised ribs. The game had barely begun but Green Bay was already seven points behind and had lost its quarterback.

Unlike Baltimore, the Packers still had a healthy backup quarterback. Zeke Bratkowski replaced Starr. Late in the first quarter, he guided the team close enough to the Colts' goal for Don Chandler to try a forty-seven-yard kick. The field goal missed. When Lou Michaels kicked one in the second quarter, the home forces were trailing 10 to 0.

Chandler was another of Lombardi's bargain basement acquisitions. With Hornung no longer able to kick with his former accuracy and Kramer hurt, the coach gave the Giants a third-round draft pick for the veteran kicker. They had known each other in New York, but Chandler admitted that when he arrived in Green Bay to renew the acquaintance his hands were sweating and he kept thinking: "If you make one mistake, you've had it."

Don was a rookie in 1956 and Vince was the Giants' offensive coach when they first met. He and another young fellow, Sam Huff, decided they'd never make the team and left for the airport, closely pursued by Lombardi. He caught them before their plane arrived.

"It's silly to go home when you haven't had a shot at it yet," he told them, and they went meekly back to the practice field, located in Winooski, Vermont.

Both had become stars. But by 1965, Chandler was considered expendable. The Packers made full use of his talents. During the season, he made seventeen of the twenty-six field goals he attempted. His replacement with the Giants, it might be noted, had a record of four out of twenty-five.

Each day before the playoff, the Packers had found the same message taped to their lockers: "Anything is ours providing we are willing to pay the price." But the inspirational wisdom did not seem to have inspired them to the extent of getting some points on the scoreboard. The half ended with the score still 10 to 0.

They had come close. Bratkowski had engineered a drive that put the ball on the Colts' one-yard line. Hornung and Taylor had each had a turn at trying to move the ball the necessary three feet. Each had failed. Then on third down, Zeke fumbled, Baltimore recovered, and even the chance for a field goal was gone.

The ground game was sputtering, but Bratkowski and his ends were doing well. Before the afternoon was over, the substitute quarterback would connect with twenty-two passes for 248 yards, with no less than eight of them caught by the former Washingtonian, Anderson. Carroll Dale, who had been acquired from the Rams before the season began, made a leaping catch in the second half that led to the Packers' first score, with Hornung bulling over for a touchdown.

Late in the game, a Green Bay drive bogged down on the Colts' twenty-two-yard line. Chandler trotted in with the field goal unit. His kick barely wobbled between the uprights. Baltimore partisans protested but the three points counted, and the fourth quarter ended with the score 10-10 and the Packers trying desperately to get lined up for another field goal attempt from the forty-six.

The game was for the division title so it could not end there. The fifth quarter began. The team scoring first would win. A few minutes later, Baltimore had the ball on the Packers' thirty-seven. Michaels began warming up on the sidelines and Matte made plans to get the ball closer to the goal. But when he handed the ball to Lenny Moore, the Green Bay line came roaring in and the play lost a yard. Taking no chances with a fumbled handoff, Matte carried the ball himself on the next play. He lost two yards. It was only third down, but Baltimore was moving in the wrong direction and Michaels came in to kick before any more ground was lost. His attempt was short and to the right.

So now it was Green Bay's turn. In the huddle a few moments later, Bratkowski indicated he was planning a pass to Anderson. Bill said that suited him just fine, and when the ball came his way he caught it for an eighteen-yard gain. It was only after the game was over that his teammates realized he hadn't known what was going on since midway in the fourth quarter when he was knocked groggy. He never remembered the over-time period at all, but his friends assured him he'd played very well.

"You run the plays so often you just go out and do it automatically," Anderson explained.

Lombardi had been saying that all along, although he preferred to have his players remain conscious while they were running around the field catching passes.

Dale caught another pass as Bratkowski moved his team to a succession of three first downs. Hornung was injured now. In his place was Elijah Pitts, who had felt so lost and lonely in his rookie year that Paul had gone out of his way to befriend him. Now Pitts was carrying the ball and he picked up four yards on second down.

On the sidelines, Lombardi turned toward Chandler.

"Field goal," he ordered.

Don started on the field, but the coach had second thoughts.

"Hold it," he shouted, and Chandler moved off the field again.

It was third down and Taylor took the hand-off.

"Don't fumble it," Lombardi yelled. "Don't fumble it."

Jim may not have heard the advice over the sound of the crowd, but he didn't fumble. He pushed and shoved and snarled his way to the eighteen and now it was fourth down and Chandler was on the field. So was Starr, who held the ball. The kick was good. Green Bay had won the longest game ever played in the National Football League.

Lombardi felt limp. Gambling on that final run to get the ball in better field position had taken a lot out of him.

"Suppose Taylor had fumbled," he said. "I'd have kicked myself all over Green Bay."

After that playoff, meeting the Browns was almost an anti-climax. Even during Green Bay's less successful years under Lombardi, his team seldom lost to a member of the Eastern Division. Still, Cleveland had such assets as Jimmy Brown, and Lombardi said he considered him "the greatest player of all time."

Starr, Hornung, Taylor, and Boyd Dowler were hurting but not enough to stay on the sidelines in a championship game. By the end of the week, it was apparent that the quarterback's bruised ribs wouldn't keep him from throwing. But, as his coach explained later, "The question was whether he could stand up under a blow in the same area."

Soon after the game began in Green Bay, several Cleveland tacklers were thoughtful enough to explore this question, hitting the quarterback hard on the right side, the location of his injury the previous Sunday. If it hurt, he didn't let on.

As for Dowler, who had been nursing a variety of injuries all season, he caught five passes during the afternoon. The Browns had noted that Anderson had caught eight the week before, several of them while he was still conscious, and they concentrated on stopping him, which left Boyd open.

In preparing for the game, Lombardi had urged his minions to control the ball. As long as they had the ball, he pointed out, it would be difficult for Jim Brown or any other Cleveland representative to score. They followed his instructions. The Browns had thirty-nine plays from scrimmage and the Packers controlled the ball on sixty-nine.

Even the Green Bay weatherman outdid himself. He provided four inches of snow the morning of the game, followed by rain, then snow again. The footing was uncertain, to put the matter mildly.

"I was running into people I'm usually able to avoid," was what the sportswriters said Jim Brown had said, and Taylor agreed that conditions underfoot were not ideal.

"You had to run cautious," he said. "You couldn't cut."

Green Bay's defense was especially impressive in the second half, holding Cleveland to 15 yards rushing and 11 yards passing. Meanwhile, the Packers totaled 174 yards during those two quarters and pulled away to a 23 to 12 victory.

When the game was over, Lombardi explained Starr's winning technique.

"He outlooked them," he said. "That's what we call it, 'outlooking.' He'd look to the left, and then throw to the right, or vice versa.

"It amuses me how many people say that Starr can't throw the long pass. I'd.like to have a nickel for every bomb he's exploded.

"Starr is one of the most underrated men in the league."

Only twenty-two of the forty men on the squad had played for the Packers in 1962, the last championship year. The players voted to have championship rings as the official memento of the 1965 season. That meant that some veterans would have three such rings, but it was felt that the newcomers would want one.

The experts were no longer talking about the Packers' being over the hill. Now they were discussing the "Packer dynasty," particularly after Lombardi dipped deep into the treasury and came up with the nation's two most publicized draftees, Donny Anderson and Jim Grabowski. One reporter dared to ask the coach if there ought to be a move to break up the Packers. Luckily, he was in a good mood.

"No," he said, giving out with that laugh that could stop traffic. "Let's break up the Bears. Let's break up Gale Sayers and Dick Butkus."

Chapter 15

The First Super Bowl

The team that critics had written off several years before as over the hill had won in 1965 mostly on what Lombardi called "character," a mixture of experience, pride, and the ability to tap a reservoir of old skills when the vernal scent of money was in the air. But as he looked toward the 1966 season, the coach understood that reinforcements were needed.

At thirty-one years old Jimmy Taylor no longer ran with quite the abandon of a few years back. Max McGee was thirty-four. Hornung was thirty, Starr thirty-two. Others who had been with Lombardi since he came to Green Bay were feeling their age, although some of them—most notably the quarterback—had managed to compensate for the added years by the skills that came with experience.

Still, the career expectancy of a football player is relatively short, and it was obvious to the coach that he needed an infusion of young talent. He had it out with the Packers' general manager, a conference that took place within the confines of his own mind.

The general manager was a businesslike fellow who had been grumbling for years about the ridiculous amounts of money that professional football clubs spent for untried rookies. The coach, on the other hand, wanted the best men available, and hang the price. For once, Coach Lombardi won the argument with General Manager Lombardi, and in the draft that preceded the 1966 season the Packers got a reputation as big spenders.

The established NFL and the younger AFL were in the final campaign of a bitter war fought with checkbooks. In 1966, the leagues persuaded Congress to grant a partial exemption from the antitrust laws so there could be a common draft of talent, thus avoiding the expensive competition. That was the start of a flirtation between the rivals that would soon lead to marriage.

Meanwhile in one last bidding battle Green Bay came up with its two most valuable prizes. The estimate most favored for the price paid for two rookies, Donny Anderson and Jim Grabowski, was a million dollars. Anderson was to become the future's Hornung, and Grabowski was to take the place of Taylor, permitting the hope that the Packer dynasty would go on forever.

The estimated cost of acquiring the two players—$600,000 for Anderson, $400,000 to keep Grabowski from joining the New York Jets— is subject to interpretation and some skepticism, but it is certain that spending anything like those amounts was painful for Lombardi, who had once worked his heart out for $22 a week. But the Packers had the money now, and the general manager was willing to spend it.

A million dollars was more than the club had grossed before Lombardi arrived, but now it was prosperous. Television revenue no longer depended on the size of each team's potential audience. The rules had been changed so that the league's smallest city got the same share of the pie as its biggest. And the pie was growing steadily in size, reflecting the soaring audience on Sunday afternoons.

The number of paying spectators had risen, too. The Packers had enlarged their stadium, but a fan might have to wait for years for the privilege of buying a season ticket. The club's annual income had climbed to around the five million dollar mark. None of the 1,698 stockholders was entitled to dividends, so the profits could be used to improve the business. And the purpose of the business was to win another championship.

The big money going to rookies made some of the veterans restless. Taylor, who recognized his playing days were not unlimited, demanded a contract that Lombardi felt amounted to an annuity. He turned him down, as he had once turned down Jim's suggestion that he be paid so much per yard gained. Taylor decided to play out his option, which meant that 1966 would be his last year in Green Bay.

The word got out. An Associated Press reporter, Ken Hartnett, did his job and wrote an article saying that the fullback had not signed a contract. The coach angrily ordered that Hartnett be barred from the team's dressing room, but AP carried the matter to Pete Rozelle and the coach was overruled.

A few months earlier, Ray Nitschke had told another reporter that he was playing out his option.

"They're paying the rookies too much and forgetting the veterans. I think I'm worth more money," he said.

Lombardi wouldn't confirm what Ray had said.

"Nobody on this ball club plays out his option until he has talked to me the last time," Lombardi said.

When the story was printed, the coach fumed about the disloyalty of the press. Nitschke soon signed, but Taylor refused, which was a violation of a Lombardi rule about what should matter to his players: "Your religion, your family, and the Green Bay Packers." Sometimes, it was said, perhaps unjustly, that Vince got the order reversed.

As one of the richest of rookies, Anderson reported to the 1966 training camp in a glow of national publicity, but he soon learned life could be hard even for a young man with all that money in the bank. In one of his first sessions on the practice field in the hot sun, he developed a mighty thirst.

"Where can you get a drink of water around here?" he asked a veteran.

"There hasn't been any water around here in eleven years," the other player told him.

Because one problem in 1965 had been that the offensive line permitted enemy tacklers to get at Starr too often, the coach gave a high priority to strengthening it. One of its members was Steve Wright, whose talents included an ability to shed criticism without worrying about it. One afternoon, his voice hoarse from yelling, Lombardi lost his precarious grip on his temper, rushed out on the practice field, and began flailing away at Wright with his fists.

Steve was fifty pounds heavier and eight inches taller. After he'd cooled off, it occurred to Vince that if Wright had brought down his fists he could have driven him into the ground like a tent peg. But the tackle did not fight back, merely warding off the blows until the coach tired and calmed down.

The fact that Lombardi had the full authority to hire and fire might have had something to do with the lineman's pacifism but the coach had another explanation.

"He understands me. Fortunately, all the Packers understand me."

In analyzing the incident, Lombardi noted that even while he was pummeling Wright he was fond of him. The tackle was one of the most likeable men on the squad, he said, and that was his problem. He had the size, he had the ability, "but he loves everybody.

"In a game, they beat on him. Everybody whacks him, and he laughs. I guess I was trying to get him to hate me enough to take it out on the opposition, because to play this game you must have that fire in you.

"And there is nothing that stokes that fire like hate. I'm sorry, but that's the truth."

Red Blaik had said something similar when Lombardi was his assistant at West Point. "To beat Navy," he had told his cadets, "you have to hate Navy." But Lombardi had understood this theory as far back as St. Cecelia's. When he was a combination coach and teacher there, one of his closest friends was Red Garrity, who coached basketball at Englewood High. They played duplicate bridge together—a true test of any friendship. They liked each other and respected each other's abilities. But on the morning of a Sunday when a game was scheduled between the two schools, if they met in church they wouldn't even say hello.

Winning the championship had not eased the pressure—rather, it had intensified it. This was the season when the champions of the two leagues were to meet for the first time in what would be called the Super Bowl, and Lombardi wanted his team to carry the NFL banner that day. And so he drove veterans and rookies alike, following the axiom of his old friend, Tim Cohane, which held that the perfect football coach should be named Simple Simon Legree, a jesting remark with much truth in it.

The Packers' resident genius felt it was more important to have his players' confidence than their affection. But somehow—for some of them, not all, and then only sometimes—he had both.

One problem that did not affect the Packers under Lombardi was the one involving race, an ancient division in the land that was much in the news in 1966. On some teams in the league black players felt subtle touches of discrimination, and some not so subtle. But Vince didn't seem to care about a man's pigmentation as long as he could play perfect football. And when he missed perfection, the coach would tell him about it at the top of his voice without caring whether his distant ancestors had lived in Africa or Europe. The explanation may lie partly in Lombardi's background—he had detected forms of discrimination against his own ancestry when he was struggling up the ladder. But mostly it was a matter of wanting the best man in each job on his team so he could win, a judgment that would only be confused by worrying about skin color.

Lombardi had long since given up his teaching career, which had never been more than a means to an end. But he had the inspired teacher's ability to conceal old truths in fresh disguises. This made him eminently quotable, not only among players but among those who make a living by writing or talking about sports.

There was, for example, his description of one of the most basic skills of football:

"If a man is running down the street with everything you own, you won't let him get away," he told his linemen. "That's tackling."

Such fundamental philosophy was taught in the 1966 training seasons, as it had been in the seasons that went before. The conditioning program was as punishing as ever, ignoring the fact that many of the players sweating and struggling on the field were now quite prosperous and famous citizens.

Lombardi and the players took pride in being called tough—he was, it was said, the toughest coach of football's toughest team, one that won a grudging compliment from a rival coach: "You always know what those goddam Packers are going to do. But you can't stop 'em. They never make mistakes."

This was not quite true, as Lombardi pointed out over and over again. Still, they seemed to make fewer errors than other teams, and before the season began Lombardi predicted that the 1966 squad would be "the best team I ever coached."

The Packers wrapped up the division title well before the season was over, their fifth in eight seasons under Lombardi. Taylor might be past his prime, but he gained 705 yards on the ground that fall, plus another 331 yards on pass receptions. Hornung had a pinched nerve in his neck—on the sidelines, the coach winced when Paul was tackled but he showed flashes of his old skills. Elijah Pitts scored ten touchdowns, playing in Paul's old position. Anderson and Grabowski played enough to gain experience and showed promise of being worth the investment the team had made in their futures. As for Starr, he was no less than brilliant and it was almost a forgone conclusion that he would be voted the league's most valuable player. He completed 156 passes out of 251 attempts, gaining a total of nearly one and a third miles.

With one game to go, the Packers had come within four points of an undefeated season and had a record of 11-2. The finale with the Rams seemed meaningless. The players were looking forward to the league championship game against Dallas and then, if they whipped the Cowboys, taking on the AFL champion in the first Super Bowl.

The Los Angeles game meant very little to anyone, with a single important exception. Detecting signs of slackening off among his players, Lombardi had them doing wind sprints and pushups before the Rams game while he stood on the sidelines yelling:

"You don't have any pride. All you have is shame. You're a disgrace to the National Football League."

In the dressing room as the players prepared to go out and face Los Angeles, the coach was so worked up that he could hardly talk. The Packers had won their divisional title, but the Rams, by winning, could place higher than they had in years. So the odds makers had made Green Bay the underdogs.

Lombardi finally found words. Neither religion nor football was ever far from his mind, and he managed to combine the two in his pep talk.

"If you give me anything less than your best," he said, hoarsely, "you're not only cheating yourself, your coaches, your teammates, everybody in Green Bay, and everything pro football stands for. You're also cheating the Maker who gave you that talent." He paused, staring hard at them, the look that had once unnerved opposing players when the Fordham Rams crouched, ready to spring. "I know we don't have cheaters on this ball club."

In describing that afternoon some years later, Bart Starr said he had never been prouder to be on a team.

"The game meant nothing, yet it meant everything," he went on. "We charged out and whipped the Rams. Sometimes I think no game we ever played for Coach Lombardi gave him as much satisfaction as the one we didn't have to win but did."

Starr was not the quarterback in that game. Bratkowski, who had started only six previous games for the Packers and won all six, kept his winning percentage intact, but it was not easy. He completed thirteen passes for 245 yards and one touchdown. Donny Anderson scored another, his second of the year. Bob Jeter helped the team tie an NFL record by running back a pass interception for a touchdown, the sixth time a Packer had accomplished that during the season. The final score was

27 to 23, the gamblers who had underestimated the Packers were foiled, and when the game was over the coach permitted himself a small smile.

"We are in the money now," he said.

The big money would go to the Super Bowl winner, however, and before the Green Bay players could collect that loot they had to get past Dallas and the Kansas City Chiefs. It was widely assumed in those days that no AFL team really belonged on the same field as an NFL team, so the chief obstacle seemed to be the Cowboys, coached by Vince's former colleague in New York.

The day before the game with Landry's team, Lombardi showed his men a new play variation—he liked to save something special for the final practice to keep them from taking life for granted—and Pitts made thirty-two yards with it on the first play of the game. But the Cowboys had some tricks in the sleeves of their jerseys, too, and both teams scored freely. One of the Dallas touchdowns could be blamed on Tom Brown, considered by Lombardi to be "a good player who is going to be a better one." He slipped and fell down, permitting the score.

With seventy-four seconds to play, the Packers were ahead by one touchdown—34 to 27—and it was fourth down. But the Cowboys had the ball on Green Bay's two. A touchdown would tie the score, perhaps send the game into overtime.

Don Meredith faked a handoff to his backs, then moved to his right, intending to pass or run as opportunity arose. Dave Robinson sliced behind a Dallas guard. He warded off a blocker. He bore down on the quarterback and grabbed him, but Meredith was able to get the ball away in the direction of the end zone.

Brown had been the goat of one play, but he was the hero this time. He grabbed the ball and the Packers' debut in the Super Bowl was only two weeks away, time enough for every NFL owner to telephone Lombardi and point out that the league's prestige was squarely on the line.

This did not come as news to Vince. He announced a new schedule of super penalties for violation of pre-Super Bowl protocol. Violating the 11 P.M. curfew would cost $2,500 instead of the usual $500. A player caught with a woman in his room would be fined $5,000. There was resentment among the players. Some of them felt hurt that the coach thought such unusual emphasis on after-hours decorum was necessary for a game that meant not only prestige but $15,000 to each winner.

"It was the biggest game of our lives," Max McGee said. "We were not about to break any rules."

Lombardi and his assistants were not sure what to expect from the Chiefs. This was the first game played between representatives of the rival leagues, and it was hard to tell how good Kansas City would prove to be. The coach decided to feel his way, making adjustments as the game progressed.

The Chiefs were similarly handicapped, but it was no secret that Green Bay's traditional strength was its running game, and the AFL champions made plans accordingly. Their defense was stacked against the ground game and during the first half the tactics worked well. The second quarter ended with the Packers only four points ahead, 14 to 10.

This would never do and Lombardi said as much in the dressing room. He had already made adjustments to the Chiefs' defense, with Starr relying increasingly on passes instead of power plays, but if the NFL was really so much better than the AFL it couldn't be proved by the figures on the scoreboard.

In the second minute of the second half, the situation changed. Willie Wood intercepted a pass, and when he was finally brought down the ball was on Kansas City's five-yard line. The Packers soon scored, and for the rest of the afternoon the outcome of the game was never in doubt.

McGee, who had caught only four passes all year, was in the lineup because Dowler got hurt. Before the afternoon had ended, he had nearly doubled his year's total by catching seven, two for touchdowns. This was Max's eleventh year with the pros, but no one was likely to argue with Lombardi's contention that "this was one of his finest games."

If Kansas City had worried NFL partisans by holding the Packers to a 14 to 10 margin in the first two quarters, Green Bay relieved their minds by winning the second half 21 to 0 to make the final score 35-10. Besides the 63,036 ticket holders, the game was watched by 65 million television viewers, with not one but two networks paying a cool $2 million for the privilege of broadcasting it.

The Packers gave the game ball to the coach, and when the reporters came crowding into the tumultuous dressing room after the fourth quarter Lombardi tried to be equally gracious in answering their questions.

"They were a good team," he said of the Chiefs. "But they lacked our depth. We wore them down. We had a little more personnel than they."

But the interviewers kept goading him for a comparison between NFL and AFL football. He evaded the questions for a while but finally tired of the contest and told them and 65 million kibitzers in front of television sets what he really thought: Kansas City, the other league's champions, didn't compare with several of the teams in the NFL. Dallas, for example, was better.

"That's what you wanted me to say," he said, "Now I've said it."

As soon as he'd had time to think, he regretted the remark and was angry at both the reporters and himself.

"My game is football, not Twenty Questions," he pointed out, which was as close to an apology to AFL fans as he could manage. After all, as he had pointed out in another connection, he "may have said some wrong things—but I have never regretted them."

He held court in his hotel room for a few close friends that night, seeming relaxed and happy. He kept picking up the football his players had given him and fondling it.

If he had any regret about the most successful afternoon, it was over the failure of Hornung to play.

"He could have played and if we had really needed him, he would have," the coach said. "His neck still bothers him though, and we weren't inclined to take a chance.

"I asked him in the fourth quarter whether he wanted to get in, but he said no."

What Hornung had said was a little more poignant than that. When Lombardi invited him to go on the field, now that the game was safely wrapped up and it would be only a gesture for old times' sake, the player who had always been his favorite declined.

"No, coach," he said. "It's all over."

Chapter 16

St. Paul Helps St. Vincent

Winning the first Super Bowl was a climax to a career, and after the season of 1966 Lombardi considered retiring from coaching. A Dallas newspaper said as much, getting an indignant blast from Vince for its pains, but he later admitted that he'd given the matter some thought even before the game with the Kansas City Chiefs.

This was nothing new. Each year, when the pressure was finally off, he wondered if it was all worth it. But this time he gave the matter his serious consideration and decided to stay in Green Bay only after he'd persuaded himself that he was needed and leaving would be disloyal to the team.

For one thing, Taylor had played out his option and was leaving. For another, an expansion club would be entitled to draft some of Green Bay's players. It was unlikely that some of the veterans had another good season left in their aging bodies, and the club would need a rebuilding job if it was going to stay on top of the league.

"I didn't think it would be fair to ask somebody else to inherit all the troubles we had," said Lombardi explaining why he'd changed his mind and decided to stay on as coach.

The coach continued to hope that Taylor would stay—"We have a lot of backs, but none like Taylor," he said—but the best he would offer was the same salary as in 1966. Meanwhile, before the training season began, he returned to the Rose Hill campus in the Bronx to accept Fordham's Insignis medal for outstanding achievement.

It was an emotional occasion for a man who could remember arriving on the campus, hopeful of making the football team. Cardinal Spellman had once told him that he had put the Fordham spirit in Green Bay, and Lombardi tried to define that spirit for six hundred students who came to see the famous coach get his medal.

"Every year I try to think of a new word for it," he said. "Last winter at the Super Bowl I called it something that I have been sorry about ever since. When those tough sportswriters asked me what made the Packers click I said, 'love.'

"Now you fellows know what kind of love I meant. It was the kind that means loyalty, teamwork, respecting the dignity of another—heart power, not hate power."

Lombardi got another tribute that month of May. In an editorial in the *Catholic Herald-Citizen*, the official weekly newspaper of the Milwaukee Roman Catholic archdiocese, he was called a theologian.

Intellectuals looked down their noses at sports figures, the editorial said, but the Green Bay coach had made a theological pronouncement of great value after the Packers whipped the Rams in the last season's final game. In answer to the question of why his team had played so hard in a contest that took place after the divisional title was already won, Lombardi said:

"We have God-given talents and are expected to use them to our fullest ability whenever we play."

The editorial writer said these words contained a lesson and added, "What a world it would be if all of us respected one another with the same ferocious loyalty displayed by the Packers."

Earlier in the year, during a February blizzard, Lombardi took his coaching philosophy to a somewhat unlikely audience in New York, the American Management Association. The planes were grounded, but because the coach had promised to make the speech he took his first train ride since 1950, when he was an assistant coach at West Point.

He turned down the suggestion of getting off at Philadelphia and making the talk by telephone. "I'll be there," he promised, and so he was although his train was four and a half hours late. A police escort met him at the station and took him to the hall. Few of the thousand managers had dared walk out of the luncheon meeting before he arrived.

A Manhattan reporter described his talk as a combination of Knute Rockne, Billy Graham, and Lyndon Johnson. Leadership required mental toughness, he told the managerial group, and to have such mental toughness they needed humility, Spartanism, love, and a perfectly disciplined will.

"If we would create something," he said, "we must be something. We make a mistake unless we keep working to win, to win, to win. . . . This is an age for heroes. The test of this century is whether we mistake the growth of wealth and power for the growth of strength and character. We've weakened discipline and respect for authority and let freedom of the individual predominate."

Cynics said this was an old-fashioned home remedy for modern ailments, but it went over well with the businessmen. Some of them left the hall with fire in their eyes and a spring in their step, and if the coach had told them to grab the ball and run with it through the Dallas forward wall, they would have been willing to try.

One businessman from a small company turned to his companion when the speech ended.

"I don't know how I'll feel tomorrow," he said. "But right now I feel we can take on General Motors."

Such speechmaking might add new dimensions to the coach's reputation, but the principal problems he faced were familiar ones. They had to do with the question of molding a winning football team and, as usual, there were complications

The league had now been divided into four divisions, requiring an additional playoff before an NFL champion was chosen. Having won two championships in a row, the Packers had the opportunity of becoming the first team to win three straight since the league was split into divisions. The Packers had taken three straight titles under Lambeau in 1929, 1930, and 1931, but Lombardi was not impressed by such an example of ancient history.

"The Little Sisters of the Poor could have won then," he said. "I want that third championship. And I deserve it. We all deserve it."

Lombardi talked Max McGee out of retiring. Then he took a gamble that he was to regret. He included Hornung's name on the list of eleven Packers from which the New Orleans Saints, the league's new team, could pick three. Considering Paul's doubtful physical condition, he doubted that the halfback would be chosen.

But he was and Lombardi had to telephone him and break the news. When Hornung picked up the receiver in his home in Louisville, the coach was in tears, so overcome by emotion that he could hardly speak. Months later, he said that that day was his saddest in Green Bay.

He had no such regrets over Taylor's decision to finish his career by playing for the Saints.

"We're going to miss Paul Hornung," he said. "We will replace the other fellow."

The coach feared that the fullback's example would lead to a situation where "only the money clubs or the fun cities would have the good players." Then he didn't consider Green Bay a fun city? No, but "It's a great city," he allowed.

Anderson and Grabowski were in the wings, waiting to replace Hornung and Taylor, but they were only second-year men and Lombardi wanted more experience in the backfield. He had Elijah Pitts, who had done well in the previous season. He also had a remarkably rapid rookie named Travis Williams, but he picked up a veteran back, Ben Wilson, from the Rams.

Partly because of concern over the dynasty Lombardi had built in Green Bay, professional football changed its rules before the 1967 draft. Vince had cornered a considerable number of other teams' draft choices through shrewd trading, and he'd intended to stock up on "futures"— college boys whose original class was about to be graduated but who had another year or so of eligibility left.

The league voted to do away with such drafting of futures, which meant Lombardi had to use up all his choices for men who would report that year. Making the best of things, he ran the names and records of college seniors through a computer he had installed near his office. He came up with a strong rookie crop—center Bob Hyland and quarterback Don Horn on the first round, linebacker Jim Flanigan on the second, a defensive back named John Rowser on the third. Williams was not picked until the fourth round—he was the ninety-third man drafted by the teams— but he turned out to be a prize. For a time, it appeared that he might not make the team, but before the year was out he had scored four touchdowns on kickoff returns, a record, and was known far and wide as Green Bay's Road Runner. He averaged forty-one yards on kickoff returns for the season.

When the new players reported to the training camp at St. Norbert College near Lombardi's home in De Pere, Wisconsin, he considered another rookie, Leon Crenshaw, a good prospect if he could slim down from his original 315 pounds.

Doc Lombardi diagnosed his case and prescribed a combination of diet and calisthenics. In two weeks, Crenshaw lost twenty-five pounds. Then he collapsed while standing in the chow line and had to be carried off to the hospital. He was back the next day, doing grass drills and wind sprints.

The coach detected flab elsewhere in the lineup.

"Some of you people are fat," he informed his veterans after their first scrimmage. "You're fat in the head and fat in the body. That $25,000 you all made for winning the Super Bowl made you all fatheaded."

The $25,000 for winning the league championship and beating the AFL's challenger was only one item in the players' improved financial standing. Many of them were earning considerable sums as businessmen, real estate speculators, and television commentators. One of them, Jerry Kramer, was about to become a best-selling author, thanks to an incident of a few seasons before when a visiting writer named Dick Schaap noticed in some astonishment that the big lineman was lying on his bed reading a book of poetry.

Schaap was in the room to interview Kramer's roommate, Jim Taylor, whose admiration for poetry was minimal, but the writer squirreled away the information about Kramer. When a publisher suggested that the daily diary of a football player might be converted into a salable book, Schaap suggested a collaboration with Kramer. Jerry started carrying a tape recorder around with him, one more sign of how the once hungry Packers were interesting themselves in activities that had only a peripheral bearing on winning the next game.

Lombardi did not like all these outside activities, but he was not in a good position to clamp down. He had too many outside interests of his own, now that he was a celebrity. He had his own television show, he had written a book, he was making investments. His face was familiar not only to every football fan but to a surprising number of Americans who ordinarily paid little attention to sports.

He understood, however, that this new prosperity and celebrity had come to him and his players only because they were winners. They could remain on their high plateau only by winning again.

"We will not defend the championship," he announced. "We will fight for it."

The first game was with Detroit. The Lions won the first half, 17 to 0. In the second half, Pitts scored two touchdowns and Chandler kicked a field goal, so the game wound up as a tie, which was not quite the result Lombardi had had in mind.

Except for Chandler, who was continuing to prove Vince's ability as a trader by giving the team the kicker it had needed before he was acquired from New York, the second game would have had the same result. As it was, a forty-six-yard field goal late in the fourth quarter gave the Packers a win over the Bears. Then they won from an expansion team, Atlanta, and on the following Sunday came from behind to whip Detroit. That added up to three victories and a tie in the first four games, and Minnesota, which had lost all its games so far, was next. But the Packers had not looked like champions.

There were nights when the coach would slump in his favorite chair at home after a frustrating day and announce: "I'm going to quit." His wife had heard such talk before.

"Oh, yes?"

"What's the matter with the world today? What's the matter with people? I have to go on the field every day and whip people. It's for them, not just me, and I'm getting to be an animal."

The Vikings won, 10 to 7, scoring all their points in the final quarter. Lombardi called a meeting of the fourteen men on the squad who had been with him since 1960. They must help him with the younger men, he said.

"Frankly, I'm worried," he told them, "I just don't know what the hell to do."

If the coach was worried, then they were worried. They had never seen him react in quite this way. But the next day, he was his familiar self. He yelled at the players. He threatened to put several of them on waivers. He waved a chair over one man's head and said he'd like to hit him with it.

Life was back to normal and the Packers responded. They went on to win the Central Division title despite four losses during the season, including one to the Rams, which in retrospect it seemed they should have won.

Lombardi was being followed around by cameramen from the Columbia Broadcasting System, which was planning a post-season special on him that would pre-empt the Ed Sullivan show on a Sunday night. The CBS crew recorded the dialogue between the coach and Dave Hanner that occurred with fifty-four seconds left to play and Los Angeles trailing, 24 to 20. Green Bay's drive had stalled on its own forty-one, and it was preparing to punt.

"Do you want Don Chandler to punt?" Hawg Hanner, now an assistant coach, asked his leader.

"No! I don't want him to punt. Why the hell would I want him to punt?"

"He's a quicker kicker."

"Donny Anderson is our regular punter. The other guy hasn't been punting. Suppose he kicks a line drive and they run it back?"

Anderson's punt was blocked. The Rams scored two plays later and won the game, 27 to 24. It was not a moment Lombardi treasured, and when the CBS producer showed him the filmed segment recording his mistake he expected him to exercise his option to have it cut. Lombardi thought about it, but then he turned to the TV man and told him, "Let it go."

The Rams won their division, which meant the Packers must face them again in the first of the series of playoffs. The game would be played in Milwaukee. All week long, the coach kept goading his players with a three-word slogan: "Run to win." Starr reported later that the words became an obsession for every member of the squad.

"Run to win," they kept telling each other. "Run to win."

On the Sunday morning of the game, Lombardi revealed the source of the slogan—no less an authority on football than St. Paul, who had advised his followers in an epistle to run to win. It occurred to Kramer, still busy taking notes for his book, that "Vince has the knack for making all the saints sound as if they would have been great football coaches."

Los Angeles took advantage of a Green Bay fumble and scored the first touchdown. It turned out to be their last of the day.

Williams, remembering St. Paul's advice, broke loose and scooted down the field for forty-six yards while the heathen pursued, making a touchdown. A few minutes later, Carroll Dale caught a pass and scored another. At the half, it was 14 to 7.

Chuck Mercein, a back who hadn't been considered good enough to play for the Giants or Redskins, ran for another Packer touchdown in the second half. Williams added another and the final score was 28 to 7.

In the locker room, Lombardi started to say something to his players, broke off in midsentence with the tears running down his rugged face, then knelt down and led the team in the Lord's Prayer. No comment was heard from St. Paul, but it would be pleasant to think that he approved.

Dallas won from Cleveland in the other preliminary playoff, so last year's opponents in the championship game would meet again. Only one game away from a third league title in a row, Lombardi wanted to win more than he ever had before, which was saying a good deal. The players had various reasons for wanting a victory, too, not the least of which was money. But some of the veterans suspected that this season would be the coach's last and they resolved to send him on as a champion.

To no one's surprise, the weather in Green Bay was terrible. Even the natives admitted that the thirteen-below temperature on the day of the game was carrying the home team's advantage over those effete Texans a little too far, particularly in view of the icy wind that swept through the stadium. But no ticket-holder stayed home. They wrapped themselves in blankets, pulled on ski masks, and mushed to the stadium on the last day of 1967. In homes throughout the land, millions of other fans sat in comfort before their TV sets and envied them.

Ignoring the danger of frostbite, the Packers went about their business with workmanlike precision, and before long they had a 14 to 0 lead. But then Dallas recovered a fumble and made a touchdown. A little later, they added a field goal. When the teams went to their locker rooms to thaw at the half, Green Bay's lead had been cut to four points.

Early in the final quarter, the Dallas halfback took the ball for what looked like a run. Instead, he passed it to Lance Rentzel. The play covered fifty yards and was good for a touchdown. With a minute and a half to play, the Packers were still trailing, 17 to 14.

Green Bay had the ball on the Cowboys' thirty-yard line. In the old days, it would have been obvious what to do—hand the ball to Taylor, who would trample the foe into the frozen field, or give it to Hornung, who ran fastest when the goal line was near and crossing it meant extra dollars in the pocket.

But Taylor was in New Orleans now. Hornung was nearby—he had retired from football after the Saints acquired him, and he had come back to watch his old team play—but he was no longer eligible for Starr's handoff.

And so it was up to the New York and Washington castoff, Mercein. He took a short pass and stayed on his feet until he reached the eleven-yard line. He tried again on the next play and was stopped on the three.

Then it was Donny Anderson's turn. He made a first down on the one-yard line.

Four plays to travel thirty-six inches—if there was time for four plays. Less than a minute was left. Starr sent his backs into the line twice, and twice the opening was not large enough. The ball was only a foot away from the goal line now, but the clock was down to sixteen seconds. The quarterback called a time out.

Now it was up to Lombardi. A field goal would tie the game and send it into overtime. He was not a man who gambled for high stakes often. He had been criticized for playing conservative football. But in what might prove to be the biggest decision of his career, he chose to take a chance. Chandler and the field goal unit stayed on the sidelines.

Later, the coach explained that he felt sorry for the chilled fans and wanted the game to end, one way or another. Those who choose to believe this was his only reason may do so. At any rate, the decision was a mark of respect for his team's ability to survive extraordinary pressure, and the man now on the spot was Bart Starr.

The coach and the quarterback had worked together so long and so closely that they thought alike by now. Long forgotten were the days when Lombardi wondered if Bart's attitude was tough enough to survive in this game for madmen. It is perhaps significant to note that now that the chance for a third straight championship depended on the next play, Starr decided he would carry the ball himself.

Kramer and Ken Bowman were to open a hole in the Dallas line big enough for the quarterback to squeeze through. That meant they would have to move Jethro Pugh and Pugh was not likely to cooperate a bit.

Then the ball was snapped, Starr gripped it, and the two lineman slammed into big Jethro. Just enough daylight was showing, and the ball was over the goal.

It was a finish to the season that will be talked about as long as football is played in Green Bay. It made the Packers' second Super Bowl, a routine victory over Oakland, an anticlimax.

In the bedlam that was the Green Bay dressing room after the Dallas game, television cameras peered at Kramer as he summed up his feelings.

"There's a great deal of love for one another on this club," he said, echoing the coach's remarks on a similar occasion. But then he went on to say, "Perhaps we're living in Camelot," and to give tongue to how he felt about Lombardi.

"Many things have been said about Coach and he is not always under-stood by those who quote him. The players understand. This is one beautiful man."

Chapter 17

Philosophy According to Lombardi

Less than nine years before, Vince Lombardi had been consigned to the obscurity of an assistant coach's job. Now he was the most widely known American sports figure since Babe Ruth.

Intellectuals took him seriously enough to argue about his philosophy of football. The most casual fan had an opinion about the Lombardi techniques and was willing to expound on it at considerable length. Around Green Bay and the rest of Wisconsin he was regarded as larger than life size, but this feeling was not confined to the geographic area that was the natural base of support for the Packers.

Lombardi stories were a staple of the humor of the day. There was, for example, the one about the football player who died and went to heaven. He noticed a team of angels scrimmaging on a celestial gridiron while a short, stocky figure stood on the sidelines and yelled insults at them.

"Who's that?" the newcomer asked St. Peter.

"Oh, that's God," the saint told him. "He thinks He's Vince Lombardi."

As one favorite gag of luncheon speakers went, the coach had been injured while taking a walk—he'd been hit by a motorboat as he strolled across the Fox River. Then there was the story about how he came home one chilly night and went to bed.

"God, your feet are cold," his wife is supposed to have said, while her husband answered: "Around the house, dear, you may call me Vince."

As with most humor, there was an underlying vein of hostility as well as admiration in such allusions to the coach. Still, Lombardi generally enjoyed the stories. He was not above telling one himself if the mood was right, laughing louder than anyone else when he came to the punch line.

"I don't care what people say about me as long as I win," he said. "That's what I get paid for."

He could hardly have been pleased by some of the nicknames given him—for example, "the Jap" because of his grin and "il Duce" because of his dictatorial methods—but he didn't mind the remark one of his players made about what would have happened if Vince had been in charge of the Italian army during World War II—Italy would have won.

There were jesting remarks about Lombardi's talents being wasted as a football coach. With the 1968 presidential election in the offing, there was talk of running him for high office—governor of Wisconsin, perhaps, or senator. The talk may have begun as idle barroom chatter, but a considerable number of people soon began to take it seriously. After all, why wouldn't it be a good idea to let him run the state—or, better still, go down and straighten out all those politicians in Washington? There were rumors that he would replace J. Edgar Hoover as boss of the FBI, so he could end crime in the streets and elsewhere. One report, which seems to have had some factual basis, had certain influential Republicans considering him a likely possibility as a vice-presidential candidate despite his lifelong habit of voting Democratic.

Vince was aware of the rumors, but he does not seem to have taken them seriously. Politics was not his game, he felt, and his chances of making a successful transition to this new field would be about the same as those of a congressman trying out for the Packers' backfield. In his own field, Lombardi knew, he was a pro, but in politics he would be an amateur and the professionals of that business would eat him alive.

One reason for the suggestions that the coach might be just what American politics needed was his habit of making speeches that appealed to a considerable element of the electorate—those who felt the country had somehow gone wrong, that things were getting out of hand, and a return to the virtues of a simpler time was long overdue.

Perhaps without intending to, he became the spokesman for the kind of people who rode around in cars bearing bumper stickers reading, "America—Love It or Leave It." His own philosophy was not that simplistic. He was too complicated a man to fit comfortably into a pigeonhole in the ideological rolltop desk, but he did feel that too much attention was being paid to the rebellious and not enough to those who went about the difficult business of keeping things from falling apart.

"It is hard to have patience with a society that has sympathy only for the underprivileged," he said. "We must have sympathy for the doer, too. We speak of freedom. Sometimes I think we confuse it with license.

"Everything is done to strengthen the rights of the individual, at the expense of responsibility to church, state, and authority. We are in the midst of a rebellion, a struggle for the hearts and the souls and the minds of all of us. . . . We do not regret the rebellion, but perhaps the battle was won too well.

"We must help the underprivileged, certainly. But let us also respect success."

Lombardi said that society should sympathize with and help the misfits, the maladjusted, the criminal, and the loser.

"But I think it's also a time for us to stand up and cheer for the doer, the achiever, one who recognizes a problem and does something about it, one who looks for something extra to do for his country—the winner, the leader."

He used such old-fashioned words as humility, sacrifice, self-denial, and even love in describing what traits were needed. He told audiences that "football is the only thing I know to talk about," but, understandably, they did not take him at his word. To an increasing extent he saw football as a symbol of larger issues and contended that the attributes that made a good football team—that is, the Packers—could be applied to other aspects of society.

There was room for argument about this, of course, and the arguments duly occurred. Lombardi was attacked as well as praised and defended, although he spoke from a position of strength: He was a winner, the king of a special sort of hill, so that even those who did not agree with him paid attention when he spoke.

During each Sunday afternoon of the recent seasons, millions of Americans had crouched in front of a magic tube on which upholstered figures knocked each other down or broke free for triumphal runs. In a world increasingly made of plastic, these young men were using bone and sinew to strive toward an easily understood goal, with the results being either victory or defeat. During a period of confusion and growing discontent, they symbolized such traditional qualities as teamwork, the need to rise above adversity, and a healthy simplicity of purpose.

They were symbols and Lombardi was their most prominent spokesman. One commentator in a highbrow journal called him the legitimate folk hero of a quiet mass movement—a movement that "tells us much about our sense of what we have lost and our sense of what we need."

And so when this celebrated folk hero stepped down as coach of the Green Bay Packers on February 1, 1968, it seemed to millions of Americans that an important era in the history of their times had ended.

There had been hints that he would retire from coaching after the 1967 season, but few of his players believed the rumors until two days before the second Super Bowl game in Miami.

"This may be the last time we'll be together," he told them. Then this tough coach, who was part softy, lost control of his emotions and left the rest of his statement dangling.

They could not be sure he would quit coaching. He had talked of resigning before and had not done so; besides, maybe his hint that the second Super Bowl would be his final game was a psychological ploy to make sure his players would go out and smite the AFL's chosen representatives into the Florida dust.

After the game was won, Lombardi denied he had made up his mind to quit.

"All these stories just might keep me coaching," he said. "I really don't know."

His Packers had won five NFL titles, the last three in a row. They had won the only two Super Bowls yet played. There were still challenges—four titles in a row would be even better than three—but at the age of fifty-four Vince was tiring of the emotional peaks and valleys that came in seemingly endless succession during the season, the necessity to drive himself so he could drive his men. Besides, the general manager's job was growing more demanding. It involved the operations of a four million dollar business now.

Finally he made his decision: to keep the less interesting and less difficult of his two roles. It was as if Robin Hood had announced he was going to subdivide Nottingham Forest or Paul Bunyan had chosen to retire from lumbering—at least that's how it seemed to Green Bay fans. As for the followers of the Bears, the Cowboys, the Rams, and the other teams that had been trailing the Packers during most of Vince's tenancy as a professional coach, any regrets they might have felt were counterbalanced by the realization that Lombardi's departure from coaching might signal the end of the recent Green Bay monopoly on first place.

The general manager chose Phil Bengston to succeed him. As coach of the defensive team, Bengston was thoroughly schooled in the master's methods. Lombardi intended to give him the same free hand he had always demanded for himself. If there were any doubts about how it would feel to stand aside and let another man handle the team, Vince was able to shove them roughly aside and keep busy.

He negotiated contracts with players. He spent considerable time with league matters, serving on the NFL committee representing the owners in a dispute with their muscular hired hands. He had a chance to play golf now and then, spend more time with his family. There was the familiar duty of fending off reporters' questions about whether his departure as coach might be merely the first step in a plan to leave Green Bay.

"This is not a utopia," he told them. "Nothing is. If the opportunity presented itself for me to get some equity, then that would be a different position entirely. But I haven't heard of any angels ready to give anything away."

His friends found him more relaxed. He told some of them that if he had his life to live over again he might have preferred to be a college coach. Still, he said, pro football had been good to him.

"I have enough material wealth to take care of Marie and my children," he told one confidant. "Now I'm continuing in football to take care of my grandchildren."

Besides running the Packers' front office, he had a new part-time career as a businessman. He became board chairman of a Madison (Wisconsin) building company, Public Facilities, Inc., a connection that would bring him a gain estimated at a million dollars when the firm was sold.

Led by a businessman named Norm Chernick, Green Bay residents made plans to honor the city's best-known resident. August 7, 1968, was Lombardi Day and it was a long and lively one.

As had so many other days during his career, it began in a church and concluded in a sports arena. Bishop Aloysius Wycislo led the 7:30 A.M. religious observance in Resurrection Church in the nearby community of Allouez. After breakfast, there were ceremonies at an intersection near Lambeau Field, with one of the streets renamed Lombardi Avenue. Mayor Donald Tilleman unveiled a special street sign, noting that after two days of rainy weather the sun was shining. Turning toward the beaming guest of honor, he added, "I don't know if it was by design or command."

The Lombardis rode to the dedication in style in an open convertible behind a color guard and the Ashwaubenon High School Band. Afterward, there was the obligatory press conference. Under questioning, Vince said he'd been approached to run for a state office but had given the proposition a "quick no." As for his future with the Packers, his immediate plans were to go on being the general manager, but "I can't predict the future." Had he ever dreamed, as a boy in Sheepshead Bay, that some day a street would be named for him?

"Yes." He paused, flashing that stainless steel grin. "Broadway."

Many of his old friends from the East were in Green Bay for the occasion—Father Tim Moore of St. Cecelia's, Pete Carlesimo of Fordham, and a number of others. They all had lunch together and Vince took their picture.

In the evening, fifty-five hundred fans turned up at the Brown County Arena and several hundred others had to be turned away. Ten of the rival football teams had sent representatives. Washington and Wisconsin politicians were on hand. A number of Vince's old friends gave speeches, including Paul Hornung. He not only praised Lombardi but had a word of reassurance for the Green Bay fans.

"The Packers are destined to win a fourth straight title," he told them. "In fact, I'll bet on it."

All in all, the day was a grand climax to Vince's career in Green Bay, further proof that, even though the publicity mills grind most profitably for sports figures who are employed in Los Angeles or New York, a man like Lombardi could command the national spotlight in a city like Green Bay.

He had been the subject of a network television special. His own book, *Run to Daylight*, had bolstered his reputation, and Jerry Kramer's best seller, *Instant Replay*, in which Lombardi was the central figure, had made him something of a legend among football followers. The guard and his collaborator had summed up Lombardi with a widely quoted grab bag of adjectives: ". . . a cruel, kind, tough, gentle, miserable, wonderful man whom I often hate and often love and always respect."

Lombardi's own ability as a phrasemaker had helped, too. People were always quoting him. There was, for example, his explanation of why the sportswriters were mistaken when they called football a contact sport:

"Dancing is a contact sport. Football is a collision sport."

His explanation of why he had decided to retire from coaching was typical of his style of expression, not to mention his philosophy. It made the sport played on Sunday afternoons for dollars sound like considerably more than a branch of the entertainment industry.

"The pressures were so horrible. . . . The pressures of losing are bad, awful, because it kills you eventually. But the pressure of winning is worse, infinitely worse, because it keeps on torturing you and torturing you. . . .

"I felt I wouldn't be able to raise myself to the right pitch for the big games and then I wouldn't be able to raise them to their best effort. I knew I couldn't ever deceive them about it because they were an extension of my personality. So that's when I decided to get out of coaching."

Practice for the coming season began on July 15 that year. Lombardi had a date to play golf. It was Bengston's team to coach now. The general manager did not intend to interfere.

But for once the iron self-discipline broke down. Vince found he couldn't stay away. He drove to the practice field and stood there watching, feeling like an outsider. It was almost more than he could stand.

The players were out there, sweating and straining to get the muscles back into shape, and they hardly noticed the man in the white shirt and slacks on the sidelines. After more than thirty years of coaching, he had climbed up on the shelf of his own free will and it was now plain that he had made the worst mistake of his life

He did not admit it—not in public, at any rate. He was willing to confess that he missed coaching and that he had the urge to speak up when he dropped by the practice field—"but I don't." Then he would change the subject. He would talk about the new underground heating system, which, it was hoped, would keep the field in better condition to play during the rugged Wisconsin winters. He might mention the new press box he had built, the improved office quarters. But such topics were not as interesting as the ones with which he'd dealt when he had been running things on the field as well as in the front office. Most of all, he missed the contact with the players. They passed him now with no more than an impersonal word of greeting for the elder statesman he had become. Their lives were no longer wrapped up in his or his in theirs.

Before the season began, he had a soundproof cubicle built in the press box so he could watch the games in lonely splendor; here, if he forgot himself and broke his rule against yelling advice or insults to Bengston's men, no one would hear.

He tried to keep busy. He tried to stay away from the field when the practice sessions were going on. But sometimes he simply had to come and stand there, looking glum, feeling the frustrations of inactivity.

It was on one such afternoon that Henry Jordan walked by. A favorite target of Vince's sarcasm in the old days, he had sometimes annoyed the coach with his flippant remarks. Once he had even gone so far as to demand his release, changing his mind only after the coach had fixed him with an icy stare and given him the gospel according to St. Vincent: "Mister, you've found a home in Green Bay—you're going to die here."

Over the years, however, big Henry had developed a fondness for Lombardi and now he had a question to ask. It went directly to the heart of the matter that was bugging Vince, and it was made partly in jest and partly in earnest.

"Coach," Jordan said, looking down at the stocky man on the sidelines, "wouldn't you like to chew us out just once more for old time's sake?"

Lombardi managed a laugh. But the question had come uncomfortably close to the truth.

Chapter 18

Washington's New Messiah

When word reached the bars and soda fountains, the clubs and family rooms, all the places where Green Bay Packers fans met to while away the time until the next season, the gloom rose like fog in the wintry air.

"Well," one beer drinker said, staring at his glass, "God is dead."

Vince Lombardi, who had roared in from the East just ten years before to rescue a team in deep distress, was leaving. The man who had talked so often of loyalty was breaking his five-year contract with the Packers.

It could have been worse. If he had gone to the Bears or Detroit or the Vikings, the shock and disappointment would have been a little greater. But it was deep enough, even though his new team, the Washington Redskins, had never loomed as much of a rival to the representatives of the city on the Fox.

Some harbored deep resentment, others said Lombardi had earned the right to do as he damned well pleased. Then there were the philosophers, such as the fan who pointed out: "Sure we named a street Lombardi Avenue and now he's gone—but they put Washington's picture on a dollar bill and he isn't around any more either."

Searching hard for a silver lining, some of the Green Bay citizens in that February of 1969 saw Vince's departure as a good omen for the team Phil Bengston would no longer have to coach in the shadow of the master. The 1968 record was testimony of how difficult the transition of authority had proved. For the first time since the head coach had been named Scooter McLean, the Packers had lost more games than they won. It seemed unlikely that they'd do worse than their 6-7-1 record even if Lombardi was no longer the general manager.

A number of theories were advanced as to why this man who had summed up his philosophy as "to win, to win, to win . . . !" chose to risk his reputation with a set of perennial losers like the Washington Redskins. In each of the last fourteen years, the representatives of the national capital had won fewer than half their games and there was considerable doubt whether even Lombardi could change that habit.

Large amounts of money were involved, it was said. But as Vince had pointed out, he already had money. A chance to buy a minority interest of the club's ownership was important—no such option was available in Green Bay because of the peculiar nature of the ownership there and Lombardi had often said he'd like to be an owner. Still, how could he possibly have a greater degree of control than he had enjoyed as a hired hand in Green Bay?

Some people said Vince wanted to move back closer to his ancestral roots in the East. But he had turned down other offers from that direction, some of them when his ties with Green Bay were newly formed.

It seems probable that a number of considerations were involved in his decision to leave the Packers, but the basic one was simple enough: He wanted to coach again and he could not coach at Green Bay without shoving aside the man he had chosen to succeed him. He came close to saying as much, although he was less specific about who would be hurt.

He would have preferred to go back to coaching at Green Bay, he said, "if there'd been a graceful way to go back without murdering a lot of people."

As long as he stayed retired, his coaching reputation was safe—141 victories in 184 games. As people kept saying, a record like that made him a legend. But that was not what he wanted.

"I'm not a legend because I don't want to be a legend," he said. "You have to be Halas to be a legend. George Halas is seventy-four years old and he's done something for the game. I'm too young to be a legend."

Like the Packers of old, the Green Bay management displayed considerable grace under pressure. It would have been easy enough for the directors to shout "foul!" and make leaving difficult. If they had insisted, Vince said later, he would have stayed. But they did not.

"They could have condemned me, but they didn't," Lombardi said. "They released me from my contract when I asked. They probably understood me better than I did myself."

Leaving the Packers did not mean he was disloyal to Green Bay, Lombardi explained in an emotional farewell to the city where he had built his reputation. "I will be loyal. I will be your friend, and I hope you will be mine."

Then it was off to Washington, where he was greeted as a miracle worker. When he was asked for a reaction to the adoring reception, the crowds of hero worshippers, his face split into that Teddy Roosevelt grin.

"What the hell's a Messiah to expect?" he demanded.

As in Green Bay, he lost no time in explaining who was boss. As Edward Bennett Williams sat benignly by, the new leader told how things would be:

"I will be executive vice-president. I will coach. I will have a substantial equity. Mr. Williams will be president, but he will go back to his law practice, I guess.

"I will have control. I will have everything."

And so his neck was out, as it had been ten years earlier, except that this time he did not have a reputation to build but a reputation to maintain, which is often even harder. No one was going to underestimate him this time. No rival teams were apt to permit him to con them into giving him the kind of players in trades that he had used to help build the Packers into such a string of successes. Before he was hired, the Redskins had traded away three of their first four draft choices, so it seemed unlikely he could come up with significant reinforcements from the current crop of college players.

The team's 5-9 record the year before was not as bad as Green Bay's had been when he was hired to replace McLean, but it was hardly encouraging. The team's principal asset was its quarterback, Christian Adolph "Sonny" Jurgensen, who held the NFL records for most passes completed, most passes attempted, and most yards gained by passing in a season. But despite Sonny's talents—Washington's followers and even some neutral observers considered him the best quarterback in football—and despite all those passes he threw, the Redskins generally lost.

The Lombardi method depended on winning. All it would take would be a losing year or two and the envious wolves would begin to howl. More important, the method required the players to put up with a great deal and it seemed doubtful that they would be willing to do so unless the rewards of winning were there.

But of course Vince was not planning to lose. He did not promise a championship—not the first year—but he did promise Washington a winning season. The Redskins' hometown is accustomed to hearing promises, a principal stock in trade of its most prominent residents, but for once the citizens did not greet Vince's predictions with their usual skepticism. Few knowledgeable fans believed there was enough talent on the team to justify any but the most modest expectations for the 1969 season. Still, St. Vincent worked miracles, didn't he? When he went through his familiar routine about not planning to associate with losers, they believed every syllable.

If Lombardi started getting homesick for Green Bay as soon as he'd had a chance to evaluate his chances in Washington, he didn't let on. But he did move quickly to surround himself with familiar faces from that community. As assistant coaches he hired Bill Austin, his assistant with the Packers for five years, and Lew Carpenter, who had played for him in Green Bay. Bob Long, who had played in two Super Bowls under Lombardi before being traded to Atlanta, was brought to Washington and added to the squad. Somewhat later, so was Chuck Mercein, whom the Packers had obtained on waivers from Washington in time to help Vince win in 1967.

Lombardi reached back to his days with the Giants for two other assistant coaches. Harland Svare had been a New York linebacker when Vince was an assistant coach for the Giants. Sam Huff, whose distinguished career with the New Yorkers might never have happened if Lombardi hadn't talked him out of leaving his first training camp, not only agreed to help coach but came out of retirement to play one more season for Washington's new coach.

Tom Brown, whose pass interception had helped the Packers win their 1967 playoff with Los Angeles, was obtained from Green Bay as Lombardi kept shuffling and reshuffling the deck, trying to deal himself a winning hand. Players came and went, with no fewer than twenty-three free agents signed.

Despite the loss of those three precious draft choices in the early rounds, the coach came up with a prize. He picked a Pennsylvanian out of Kansas State, Larry Brown, on the eighth round. Before his rookie year ended, Brown nearly broke the team's rushing record and was picked for the Pro Bowl.

Lombardi spoke about how he had turned down offers from San Francisco, Boston, Philadelphia, and Pittsburgh before accepting the one from Washington, just as he had turned down other jobs before he went to Green Bay. Somehow, he said, he had known that the opportunity offered by the Packers would be right for him.

"And that's the way it was with Washington," he said, "as if the Lord's hand was on my shoulder and I knew which was the right thing to do."

His choice of old friends as his assistants was not a matter of nostalgia but simply good sense, according to his way of thinking.

"You cannot be successful in football unless you have people who bend to your personality. They must bend or already be molded to your personality. . . . I'm only one man. I can only be that one man and I've got to have men who bend to me."

Such talk would have sounded familiar enough around Green Bay, but it was different from that usually heard around Washington. That sophisticated city ate it up.

"I know a lot of what I say sounds corny out of context," the coach told one interviewer as the 1969 season approached. "It's better in the heat of the moment. But it is me.

"Hell, I'm an emotional man. I cry. I cried when we won the Super Bowl and I cried when I left Green Bay. I'm not ashamed of crying. Football's an emotional game. . . . If you're going to be involved in it, you got to take your emotions with you, mister."

He had been unhappy sitting in his soundproof refuge above the stadium in Green Bay. It wasn't so much the winning or the excitement he missed. What he had missed most was the closeness, the rapport between a coach and his men.

"For me, it's like father and sons, and that's what I missed," he said. "I missed players coming up to me and saying, 'Coach, I need some help because my baby's sick,' or 'Mr. Lombardi, I want to talk to you about trouble I'm having with my wife.' That's what I missed most— the closeness."

Others besides Lombardi compared his team to a family. Writing in the magazine *Commentary*, Richard Schickel said that Vince was working toward, consciously or otherwise, "the creation of a psychological framework much richer and more complex than a corporate leader can possibly know when he is exhorting his employees to practice team spirit.

"He was really re-creating a traditional sense of family, the kind of basic, social entity that few of us know at first hand anymore. He was an old-fashioned man, playing old-fashioned football in an old-fashioned atmosphere where he was the pater familias, demanding that his respect—his love—be earned and re-earned constantly. And it is perhaps a measure of how far we have come from the days in which this type was a commonplace to note how mysterious and exotic Lombardi seemed to sports writers and fans alike. . . ."

So, it was agreed, the Packers had been a family, with Lombardi the sometimes benevolent, often stern papa. But that had been in another time and place. This was Washington, where the coach was known only by reputation. As the time drew close for the Redskins to go into training, it seemed that the most interesting question in that city of numerous questions was what would happen when the coach's ironbound discipline clashed with the life style of the team's star quarterback.

Sonny Jurgensen had been a most successful player except for one small drawback—his teams had never won anything. At the age of thirty-five, he had played in the NFL for twelve seasons and was known for his devastating passing on the field and his lighthearted quips off it. The remark he made when traded to Washington some seasons back was still widely quoted: "When I left Philadelphia, the bartenders all wore black armbands." His comment about his 1968 coach, Otto Graham, was also not the kind that would amuse Graham's successor. "The only difference between Otto and me," Sonny had explained, "is he likes candy bars and milk shakes and I like women and scotch."

Jurgensen had picked up some weight around the middle, but he was still the league's most accurate passer. Unless he and the new coach could compromise their diverse attitudes, the Redskins would be in for some even heavier weather than usual. As Paul Hornung or Max McGee could have predicted, the compromise proved to be no problem at all. After Sonny had a talk with Vince and vice versa, he began to act like a young man who's within one merit badge of becoming an Eagle Scout. The coach had convinced him that he would be playing for a winner for a change, and it turned out that this was just what Jurgensen had wanted to do all along.

He shaved off his long sideburns—it was the coach's straight-faced claim that such unnecessary hair cut a player's speed by adding to the wind resistance. He headed straight home after work. He showed up for training camp minus ten of those excess pounds he'd carried through the previous season. He participated in the patented Lombardi program of open air torture without a murmur of complaint.

At Dickinson College in Carlisle, Pennsylvania, the Redskins' equivalent of the Packers' training camp at St. Norbert's in De Pere, Wisconsin, the coach put the players through the same agonizing grass drills with which his Green Bay employees had become so familiar. After one such session was over, he yelled at Jurgensen and Huff to lead the squad in making three laps around the field. A tackle, Ray Schoenke, said later that he'd never forget what happened next.

"Sonny looks at Huff and says, 'If you can do it, so can I.' And they're grinning! All us young guys who were thinking we couldn't take any more felt pretty silly."

Still, the conditioning was hard on such veterans as Huff, who had not intended to play any more football until Lombardi had persuaded him he had another season of good, hard hitting left in him.

One afternoon, the squad was doing wind sprints around the baseball backstop with Lombardi yelling at them: "You're like a bunch of cows. You're breathing like a bunch of cows."

"Don't breathe," other players kept telling Huff. "Don't breathe."

Sam tried, but his panting could be heard for blocks and it was a considerable time before Lombardi finally called a halt. The big linebacker dragged himself to the sidelines. Father Tim Moore, who had driven down from Jersey to watch the practice, was standing there.

"Tim," Huff said, "I'm dying."

The priest was outside Vince's office one afternoon when three nervous young men went in. Each was a rookie who had been given a sizable bonus for signing a contract by Otto Graham. Moore did not hear their side of the conversation but he learned later they had told the coach they'd decided to quit.

There was no difficulty in hearing Lombardi's reaction, however, even though the office door was closed.

"If you quit now, you're going to quit in everything you do in life," he told them. "You're going to quit on life."

The lecture went on for some time. The young men finally crept off, looking shaken, and Vince stormed out to discuss their shortcomings with Father Tim.

"They loved the game a week ago and now they don't like it," he said. "This is an example of the moral code of our country. This is what our colleges are turning out."

After he'd calmed down, he told the priest that he'd planned to cut two of the rookies from the squad anyway. But that was no excuse for their giving up on themselves, he said.

Things worked out better with that eighth round draft choice, Larry Brown, but at first it seemed unlikely that he would stay on the squad. He was an inch less than six feet tall and weighed 198 pounds, somewhat below the usual standards for professional backfield men. If he wanted to play for the Redskins, Lombardi told him, he'd have to learn to catch passes as well as run with the ball.

Brown worked tirelessly on his pass-catching, showing the kind of determination that appealed to his boss. But Lombardi noticed he kept getting the ball off late during scrimmages. He yelled at him about it and Larry kept trying to do better, but still he moved a step behind the others when the ball was snapped.

Then it was discovered that the rookie was nearly deaf in one ear. Lombardi got league approval to fit Brown's helmet with a hearing aid and from then on his play improved.

"I never had any problems hearing Coach Lombardi," Larry explained after his deafness was diagnosed. "Only the quarterback."

Once again following the pattern he had established at Green Bay, the new Washington coach paid primary attention to beefing up the Redskins' defense. In years past, Jurgensen's passing had usually given the team a few touchdowns each game, but the opposition had generally managed to score more.

Remembering a promising benchwarmer at Green Bay, Leo Carroll, Vince traded for him and made him a defensive end. A free agent from the University of Hawaii, John Hoffman, took the other end's spot, and a pair of second string holdovers from the previous season, Frank Bosch and Spain Musgrove, became starting tackles. With Huff bolstering the defense as middle linebacker and with other defensive men playing better than before, the Washington team was to develop a reputation in dealing with the long pass that led one sportswriter to claim that Lombardi had gone the local politicians one better and succeeded in banning the bomb. In the first five games of the 1969 season, the longest successful throw by an opposition quarterback went for just sixteen yards.

In the training camp, the coach emphasized contact drills more than he had at Green Bay—"I want to find out which players have the desire," he explained. The Redskins' introduction to what the Packers had called the nutcracker drill was considered quite successful. When the session was over, tight end Pat Richter had a broken nose, Schoenke wore a bandage on a damaged knee, and linebacker Roger Jarvis had a broken arm.

Someone pointed out that Washington had four times as many bars as Green Bay, but Lombardi did not see that as a disciplinary problem. Green Bay had more per capita, he pointed out truly—"There's one on every corner and two or three in between.

"We will have as few rules as we can get away with—there's no use having rules you can't enforce," he said. "For that matter, even one bar can get you in trouble."

It was noted that the Washington players looked different, even those who had been around for years. They wore ties. They were careful of their public image. They were traveling first class—a Lombardi maxim, among many—and they behaved accordingly. There were those in Washington who hoped that the team's new attitude would rub off on the politicians and bureaucrats.

"The Lombardi administration seems certain to revolutionize life in official Washington," a Washington *Post* writer predicted. "For one thing, he is dedicated to winning. He defines happiness as the achievement of one's objective. This is a radical doctrine in a government and a city where most jobs depend on seeing that no problem is ever really solved.

"If the Agriculture Department bureaucrats actually cured the farm problem or the poverty program administrators ended poverty, they would, of course, be out of work."

As the training sessions continued that summer of 1969, the coach spent part of his time studying the diverse personalities of the men who had a chance of staying with the forty-man squad when the season began. He tried to come to some conclusions about how each man would react to criticism and to pressure.

"Some can take constructive criticism in front of a group and some can't," he explained. "Some can take it privately but others can only take it indirectly.

"Football is a pressure business and on my teams I put on most of the pressure. I've got to learn forty ways to pressure forty new men."

The world had moved another ten years away from the seemingly safe and settled days of Lombardi's youth when many of his attitudes had been formed in the disciplined environment of his family, the church, the parochial school, and at Fordham. Unrest was fashionable, particularly among what was being called the now generation—an age group from which the younger Redskins were drawn. There was some doubt about how the rebels would react to the Lombardi methods, but Vince did not share it. The now generation was not quite the right title, he felt.

"I would call it the why generation. They don't want a yes or no. They're asking why. We can't have them defying authority . . . but that's not the whole story. They're raising some questions that aren't being answered."

The Establishment, of which the coach was certainly a part, was also being confronted with demands to move faster in giving blacks the rights they'd been promised a century before, and the unrest was affecting sports as well as other fields. Washington's situation was complicated by the fact that the Redskins had been the last NFL team to integrate their lineup, one of the reasons why the team had been losing for so many seasons. By the time Vince was hired to run things, Washington's locker room was no longer segregated, but blacks remembered how it had been a few years before. As was the case in Green Bay, Lombardi's attitude toward race could be summed up in a phrase he once used to describe his players: "They're all the same damn color." It was soon plain that the new coach didn't care about a man's ancestry, although he had quite decided opinions on how he should block, tackle, or run with a ball.

Once he'd decided that Larry Brown could provide half of his backfield punch now that the rookie could hear the quarterback, he needed another runner and found one in Charlie Harraway, who had done well for Cleveland in 1968 but was now expendable. The Browns had added Bo Scott and Ron Johnson to a backfield that already included Leroy Kelly, and Harraway was put on waivers. Lombardi claimed him, giving him a Redskins' equivalent of the Hornung-Taylor combination and improving Washington's running game so that its attack did not rest solely on the muscles in Jurgensen's arm.

Meanwhile, the coach yelled and cajoled, pleaded and demanded, trying to mold this team of perennial losers into winners. His reputation was on the line—"the more you've got to lose, the more nervous you get about losing it," he said—and the time was growing short, the weeks were passing, the season was about to begin.

The constant pressure being applied by the Lombardi school of applied psychology was having its effect, even on such veterans as Sam Huff.

"Just being around Lombardi," he said, "I get very nervous. I want to play, want to hit somebody. I've been with presidents of the United States and I never felt the excitement I feel with Lombardi."

Shortly before one of the practice sessions began, an assistant coach arrived with a message from the players: they'd like to postpone the start of the day's training by thirty minutes so they could watch the historic take-off of Apollo 11, which would head toward mankind's first landing on the moon. No one in Green Bay would have come up with such a suggestion, but the Redskins, thoroughly accustomed to the Lombardi molding process, had asked the question.

"What the hell good is it going to do the astronauts or our team if we sit on our fannies and watch them go up?" Vince demanded.

So practice began right on time, the seventy players who were hoping to win one of the forty jobs going through their strenuous routine while the astronauts rode away from the earth. Before the session was over, however, the coach called a halt. He gathered the men around him and gave an emotional and inspirational talk about what the astronauts were attempting. To some of the players, it almost seemed as if the moon-seekers were members of the Redskins and that their success was nearly as important as a Washington victory in the opening game with the New Orleans Saints.

When the coach had finished his talk, he and the players knelt down and Lombardi led them in a prayer for the astronauts' safety. To the surprise of none of the believers in St. Vincent's powers of persuasion, Apollo 11 performed beautifully all the way to the moon and back.

Chapter 19

A Final Tribute from the Boys

During what was destined to be Lombardi's last season in football, he threw a small and select party at the $115,000 home he'd purchased in Potomac Falls, one of the Washington area's most exclusive neighborhoods. It had two acres of grounds, four bedrooms, and five bathrooms. The suburb was described as "famous not only for the high cost of its houses but also for its rustic post and rail fences, built-in bridle paths, friendly social life, and an assortment of wealthy residents who prefer the quiet, manicured fields of Potomac to urban life."

The guest list, at least as impressive as the house, included senators, a former Supreme Court justice, and prominent sports figures. It was all a long way from Sheepshead Bay or the days when Vince had been earning $1,700 a year at St. Cecelia's. Father Tim Moore, who had hired him for that coaching job, was at the party, however, and toward the end of the evening he walked over for a chat with his host.

"You're really up there now, Vince. It's not like the old days."

"Yeah," Lombardi agreed, looking around at the well-dressed guests, the luxurious surroundings. "Yeah. But then we had a lot more fun."

The season had begun well, with the Redskins showing their familiarity with Lombardi's winning ways by beating New Orleans. The trip south had been educational for the young players for a number of reasons, one being their introduction to the coach's rules of conduct in what he considered one of the league's fun cities.

"You should have seen the list of off-limits places he handed out in New Orleans," a player confided to a magazine writer a few days later. "The only place left was the Ol' South Pancake Kitchen."

Cleveland was next, and the prospect of playing the Browns did not improve the coach's mood. The stomach trouble he was having cleared up once the team got to Ohio, however, and Lombardi seemed cheerful again. The fact that Cleveland is seldom accused of being a town for swingers may have had something to do with the change.

The game did not start well. One Lombardi detractor, noting the character of the Washington offense, claimed that the coach must have worked out a new system—putting the blockers behind the runner. Early in the fourth quarter, with a cold rain falling, the Redskins were behind, 20 to 10.

Although this trend was not much different from Washington's pre-Lombardi days, the big difference was that the team was playing as though it expected to win. The players seemed to have acquired a new tenacity, some measure of that "mental toughness" the coach was always talking about. With seventy yards to go, Jurgensen reached back into his bag of tricks, and three passes later the score was 20 to 16.

Then the Browns fumbled on their own thirteen-yard line, and Leo Carroll, a member of the contingent of former Packers who were now playing for Washington, threw himself on the ball. Jurgensen lost no time. On the next play, he threw a touchdown pass—the 196th such pass of his career—and with less than five minutes left to play the Redskins were ahead 23 to 20.

Now it was up to the defense to hold the Browns, who had the ball seventy-four yards from the Washington goal. The coach had spent a disproportionate amount of his time and energy in working with these young men whose job was to keep the enemy from gaining, but the time had been short, the talent had been below the level of his desires, and, besides, the Browns' running game was formidable. The defenders dug their heels grimly in the mud and fought back, but Cleveland marched inexorably down the field and scored with less than a minute and a half to play. The Redskins had lost a game they might have won, and it was now plain, if there had ever been a doubt, that maintaining the coach's unbroken record of winning seasons would not be easy.

Still relying on the traditional Redskins' weapon, Sonny Jurgensen's passing arm, Washington managed to tie San Francisco in the final minute of the following Sunday's game. But that only meant that the team would return to Washington for its home field opener with a record of 1-1-1.

A capacity crowd turned out, but hardly anyone was talking about winning a championship now. It had begun to seem that making winners out of the Redskins was too much even for Lombardi.

The visiting team that Sunday afternoon was from St. Louis. The Cardinals scored first, but then Sonny limbered his throwing arm, Brown found holes in the St. Louis line for good gains on the ground, and Sam Huff grabbed a pass from the Cardinal quarterback. Showing previously unsuspected speed and stamina, which reflected the training season torture, he ran it back thirty-two yards. By half time, Washington was ahead 23 to 3, and in the stadium stands the talk of Lombardi's ability as a miracle man was being happily revived.

According to well-established tradition, the Redskins could be expected to blow twenty-point leads in the later stages of the game, but it didn't happen that way this time. The final score was 33 to 17 and the momentum continued with victories over the Giants and the Steelers to make the record 4-1-1.

It was too good to last and it didn't. Washington lost its next game to the Colts, then lost another and tied one, making the statistics read 4-3-2 and ending any hope of climbing to first place. In fact, the team would have to win three of its last five games to have the winning season Lombardi had promised, and two of those games—the ones against Los Angeles and Dallas—could be written off as hopeless, considering the ability displayed by the Rams and Cowboys.

That meant that Washington must beat Atlanta, Philadelphia, and New Orleans to win more games than it lost. Atlanta was first and the Redskins won by a touchdown. They beat Philadelphia and, as expected, lost to Los Angeles. With only the New Orleans and Dallas games left, Washington had to have one more victory, and the only likelihood of getting it was to whip the Saints.

Lombardi wanted this game. He prepared for it with all the grim determination of a coach whose team is heading for the Super Bowl although, in truth, the most the Redskins could hope for now was second place in the Capitol Division and a percentage above the .500 mark.

"Second place is meaningless," the coach had said. "You can't always be first, but you have to believe that you should have been—that you are never beaten, that time just runs out on you."

But now he wanted second place and the secondary consolation of a winning season. Part of it was pride. Part of it was the feeling that he must instill an unwillingness to lose into this frustrating group of athletes so that 1970 would turn out better than the season that was ending. He drove his men as hard as he had ever driven the Packers in their days of glory and once again it paid off. Washington won from the Saints by three points and, even though the Redskins lost the season's final game to Dallas, the team had its first winning season in fifteen years. It was duly noted that the 1969 Redskins had won exactly as many games as the 1959 Packers, a team that had gone on to become the most successful in league history.

The team members found some consolation in the realization that when July came and the 1970 training season began, the survivors of the 1969 squad could report as winners. After six months of Lombardi's rule, the players preferred not to have to learn how he would react to the unfamiliar challenge of coaching his first squad of losers.

The players could relax and, if they chose, let their hair grow. Lombardi contended that long hair made the head hot inside a helmet and had once advised a rookie named Trenton Jackson, when he showed up with a mustache: "You could run faster if you didn't have that thing on your lip."

There was no off-season for the coach, however. In the interlude before the next season's work began, he had to come up with a formula for instilling in these players what he called "a ravenous appetite for success." It was an appetite that he had developed during a quarter century of waiting for his big chance, and he must make plans for creating another team in his own special image, a team that could be taught to dominate football in the seventies as his Packers had dominated the sixties.

He was realist enough to know the odds against such a repetition of history, but the challenge was there and he had accepted it. There was still time, it seemed. He would be fifty-seven on June 11, but that was not old—look at George Halas.

Lombardi had given up cigarettes in 1965, going from two and a half packs a day to none by applying his well-established theories of self-discipline. He felt the shadow of encroaching time now and then—his knee bothered him sometimes and he groused about his arthritis, but a former athlete could expect a few aches. Besides, as some of the more daring players reminded him when he was in a good mood, pain was in the mind.

One of his friends had been watching him as he stood on the sidelines during the Washington-San Francisco game the previous October and had seen him clutch his abdomen and turn white. But a few moments later he seemed to have forgotten any problems except those that his players were having on the field.

A little more than a month before the start of the 1970 training season, however, the coach began to have digestive troubles that could not be ignored. June 27, he underwent an operation in which two feet of colon were removed. Reassuring statements were issued—a tumor had been found, it was announced, but it was benign.

Lombardi, his wife, and a few others knew better, however. The enemy was cancer and he was doomed. The truth was hidden because Harry Lombardi was old and ill, and Vince did not want his father to pick up a newspaper and learn that his son was fatally ill.

Among those who knew the truth was Tim Moore, the priest who had shared in so many of his old friend's triumphs. Hurrying to Washington to be with him, he brought a bouquet to the hospital.

"Forget the flowers—who needs flowers?" Lombardi said. "But pray. Don't forget to pray for me, Tim."

Father Moore said he would pray. He found that although Lombardi was gloomy about his prospects, he was still making plans for the season. Training camp was to open in Carlisle, Pennsylvania, and Lombardi was planning to take full charge as usual. One complication was that he must return to the hospital each week for cobalt treatments, and, he told the priest, he planned to make the trips by helicopter.

The coach was permitted to leave the hospital in time to go to New York to join negotiations between the owners and the players on July 25. The players were on strike. Only the rookies were reporting to training camps. Lombardi was pale and gaunt, but he had some vigorous advice for his management colleagues:

"Gentlemen, don't give away your game to a bunch of twenty-two-year-old kids."

After the meetings, Vince and his wife went to La Guardia Field to catch a plane for Washington. Marie could see how tired he was. She asked an airline clerk to get him on the plane ahead of the crowd, but boarding was delayed and when the short flight was over Lombardi was exhausted.

His wife started carrying their two heavy suitcases through the terminal. A young man asked if he could help. In the old days—that is, a few weeks ago—the coach would have said no and perhaps felt insulted at the suggestion that a former member of the Fordham line needed assistance. But now he turned to the passer-by and said, "Help me."

"I almost cried right there," Marie Lombardi said later in describing the incident.

The next day, Lombardi went to Baltimore to see the Redskins' rookies play the Colts' first-year men. It was just another game, one of hundreds he'd watched over his years in high school, college, and with the pros. It meant very little except that this was the last one he would ever watch. He wanted to win it too. He had wanted to win all of them. But the Washington rookies lost.

Within twenty-four hours, Lombardi was back in the hospital for more surgery, a final desperate effort to win a battle that was already lost. When the coach was able to see visitors, one of the first was Father Moore. He found Lombardi forty pounds lighter. The Irishman looked down at the wasted figure in the bed and tried not to show how he felt. He leaned over to hear what Vince was saying and, for a moment, he wondered if his old friend was delirious. Here he was, facing death, and he was talking about submarines.

"How's that again, Vince?"

"I said, 'Do you know how you sink an Italian submarine?' "

"No. No, I guess I don't know how you sink an Italian submarine."

"You put it in the water," Lombardi said.

Death arrived on the third day of September, 1970. There was standing room only in St. Patrick's Cathedral in Manhattan on the day of the funeral, and several thousand New Yorkers stood quietly behind police barricades outside the church. Some came to see the celebrities, some to pay a final tribute to a hometown boy who had become great. The Packers flew in from Green Bay to attend the ceremonies. The Redskins were there. The Giants had a considerable delegation of mourners, along with players and owners and former players from other clubs in the league. In their street clothes, the shoulder pads and helmets left behind, the athletes looked smaller than on Sunday afternoons and more vulnerable, more human.

Political dignitaries were in the cathedral, along with old friends from Brooklyn, St. Cecelia's, Fordham, West Point, and other way stations on the coach's journey. Most of the men and women in the church sat staring stonily ahead as the Roman Catholic church consigned one of its faithful sons to God.

One of the younger Redskins was an exception. He had learned from last season how demanding Lombardi could be, how impatient with errors, how loud and even abusive; but now he was thinking of how much he had lost when that sometimes abrasive voice had been stilled, and during the final ritual he put his head on the shoulder of the player next to him and let the tears flow.

And why not? As the gospel according to St. Vincent had put it so often, "If you're going to be involved in it, you've got to take your emotions with you." The text had referred to football, but had not Lombardi also said that football was symbolic of life itself?

So it was all right for this muscular young man to cry for what had been lost. It seems likely that Lombardi would not only have fully understood but would have considered it a mark in his favor, both as a man and as a football player—which was, come to think of it, much the same thing in his book.

In the days between Lombardi's death and his funeral, the outpourings of tributes were unprecedented for any figure in the world of sports. To some, it seemed too much, and before long there was an occasional quibble of dissent.

After all, it was pointed out, Lombardi had been nothing more than a football coach. He had not cured the common cold or abolished poverty or solved any of the other numerous problems man is heir to. He was a fine man, no doubt, but weren't his ideas a bit old-fashioned for the seventies? He might be a folk hero, but most of those who admired him did nothing more heroic on Sunday afternoons than crouch in front of the boob tube with a six pack of beer while some paid athletes entertained them.

This type of criticism existed to a limited extent. If one of those who questioned Lombardi's credentials as a national hero had brought the matter up within the hearing of Red Blaik or Sam Huff or Bart Starr or, for that matter, Tim Moore of New Jersey, they would have been answered in a hurry, you may be sure. If they had brought it up around certain of those 209 neighborhood taverns in Green Bay, they might have had to leave without finishing their beer.

But perhaps a better answer than words was provided during the long drive the hearse and forty-six limousines made from St. Patrick's to the cemetery in New Jersey where the Lombardis had bought a burial plot when Vince was an obscure assistant in the pay of the Giants.

The procession was not planned as a parade, but as it sped through the small New Jersey towns it took on the characteristics of one. The streets were lined with people. They had been waiting for hours for this glimpse of history passing, the men and women standing with proper solemnity.

The children knew better than to wear long faces and a dignified air. They waved at the procession. They were wearing helmets, some of these New Jersey boys, and a number of them had put on shoulder pads. They were Giants fans. But they had suited up to honor a man who, within the span of their memory, had represented the enemy, the Redskins or the Packers.

Lombardi was a coach, the most successful one in professional football history. But he was a teacher as well, seeking by precept and example to show that the pursuit of excellence was relevant even in a time when the mottos most in fashion seemed to be "getting by" and "making do."

These kids in their football suits were a sign that the lesson had borne fruit, an indication that his life had been an influence on the young, the ones he had always been trying to reach.

There had been solemn eulogies that day for this man who had said that winning is better than losing and that while the losers might deserve help and sympathy it was time to remember that the winners were the builders, the ones who held the country together. The tributes came from President Nixon and other famous men.

But it was the future that had always been the coach's concern. It seems possible that the honor paid him by those kids in their Giants helmets, lining the roadsides, was the one he would have valued most of all.

Ten Seasons as a Pro Head Coach

1959 Season

Lombardi's first team as a professional head coach:

Name	Age	Position	Season in NFL
Beck, Ken	24	Tackle	First
Bettis, Tom	28	Guard	Fifth
Borden, Nate	27	End	Fifth
Brown, Tim	22	Back	First
Butler, Bill	22	Back	First
Carpenter, Lew	26	Fullback	Sixth
Currie, Dan	25	Center	Second
Dillon, Bob	30	Back	Eighth
Dittrich, John	26	Guard	Second
Dowler, Boyd	22	End	First
Forester, Bill	27	Guard	Seventh
Francis, Joe	24	Quarterback	Second
Freeman, Bob	26	Back	Third
Gregg, Forrest	26	Tackle	Third
Gremminger, Hank	26	Back	Fourth
Hanner, Dave	30	Tackle	Eighth
Hornung, Paul	24	Halfback	Third
Jordan, Henry	24	Tackle	Third
Knafelc, Gary	28	End	Sixth
Kramer, Jerry	24	Guard	Second
Kramer, Ron	24	End	Second
Masters, Norm	26	Tackle	Third

McGee, Max	27	End	Fourth
McHan, Lamar	27	Quarterback	Sixth
McIlhenny, Don	25	Halfback	Fourth
Nitschke, Ray	23	Back	Second
Quinlan, Bill	27	End	Third
Ringo, Jim	28	Center	Seventh
Skoronski, Bob	25	Tackle	Second
Starr, Bart	26	Quarterback	Fourth
Symank, John	24	Back	Third
Taylor, Jim	24	Fullback	Second
Temp, Jim	26	End	Third
Thurston, Fred	26	Guard	Second
Tunnell, Emlen	34	Back	Twelfth
Whittenton, Jesse	24	Back	Fourth
Williams, A. D.	26	End	First

The results of the season's games follow:

Green Bay 9, Chicago 6
Green Bay 28, Detroit 10
Green Bay 21, San Francisco 20
Los Angeles 45, Green Bay 6
Baltimore 38, Green Bay 21
New York 20, Green Bay 3
Chicago 28, Green Bay 17
Baltimore 28, Green Bay 21
Green Bay 21, Washington 0
Green Bay 24, Detroit 17
Green Bay 38, Los Angeles 20
Green Bay 36, San Francisco 14
Record: 7 wins, 5 losses

1960 Season
Chicago 17, Green Bay 14
Green Bay 28, Detroit 9
Green Bay 35, Baltimore 21
Green Bay 41, San Francisco 14
Green Bay 19, Pittsburgh 13
Baltimore 38, Green Bay 24

Green Bay 41, Dallas 7
Los Angeles 33, Green Bay 31
Detroit 23, Green Bay 10
Green Bay 41, Chicago 13
Green Bay 13, San Francisco 0
Green Bay 35, Los Angeles 21
Playoff game: Philadelphia 17, Green Bay 13
Regular season record: 8 wins, 4 losses
Postseason record: 0-1

1961 Season
Detroit 17, Green Bay 13
Green Bay 30, San Francisco 10
Green Bay 24, Chicago 0
Green Bay 45, Baltimore 7
Green Bay 49, Cleveland 17
Green Bay 33, Minnesota 7
Green Bay 28, Minnesota 10
Baltimore 45, Green Bay 21
Green Bay 31, Chicago 28
Green Bay 35, Los Angeles 17
Green Bay 17, Detroit 9
Green Bay 20, New York 17
San Francisco 22, Green Bay 21
Green Bay 24, Los Angeles 17
Playoff game: Green Bay 37, New York 0
Regular season record: 11 wins, 3 losses
Postseason record: 1-0

In the game in which a Lombardi team won its first national championship by beating the Giants before 39,029 spectators at City Stadium in Green Bay on December 31, 1961, the Packers failed to score in the first quarter. But four seconds after the second quarter had begun, Paul Hornung made a six-yard run for a touchdown, then kicked the point.

As it turned out, those seven points would have been plenty. It was a difficult afternoon for the New Yorkers. They made only one first down by rushing. Y. A. Tittle's twenty pass attempts were caught ten times by receivers, but four of the receivers happened to be Packers. The other

Giants quarterback, Charlie Conerly, had a better average, completing four of eight passes, but none for touchdowns.

New York added to its numerous troubles by fumbling five times. Meanwhile, Bart Starr had a ten of seventeen completion record for 164 yards and three touchdowns, and Hornung and Jim Taylor combined to gain 158 yards rushing. The Packers made eighteen first downs by rushing or passing, compared with the Giants' five.

Ron Kramer caught two touchdown passes, Boyd Dowler the other. The score was 24 to 0 at the half, 34 to 0 at the end of the third quarter. Hornung added a nineteen-yard field goal late in the game to round it out at 37 to 0.

The gross receipts at this NFL championship game were $1,013,792, with each Packer player getting $5,195.44 and each Giant player $3,339.99

1962 Season

Green Bay 34, Minnesota 7
Green Bay 17, St. Louis 0
Green Bay 49, Chicago 0
Green Bay 9, Detroit 7
Green Bay 48, Minnesota 21
Green Bay 31, San Francisco 13
Green Bay 17, Baltimore 6
Green Bay 38, Chicago 7
Green Bay 49, Philadelphia 0
Green Bay 17, Baltimore 13
Detroit 26, Green Bay 14
Green Bay 41, Los Angeles 10
Green Bay 31, San Francisco 21
Green Bay 20, Los Angeles 17
Playoff game: Green Bay 16, New York 7
Regular season record: 13 wins, 1 loss
Postseason record: 1-0

The 1962 Packers were Lombardi's most successful team in his ten seasons as a professional head coach.

Bart Starr was the league's best quarterback that year, according to statistical measurements. His pass completion record of 62.5 percent led the NFL, with 178 completions in 285 attempts for a total gain of 2,438 yards. Y. A. Tittle, the Giants' quarterback, ranked second, with a completion record of 53.3 percent. Only nine of Starr's passes were intercepted, an unusually low number. Tittle, by contrast, threw twenty interceptions.

Jim Taylor led the league in rushing, gaining 1,474 yards in 272 attempts for an average gain of 5.4. For the second straight year, the Packers gained more yards on the ground than any other NFL team, a total of 2,460. They scored thirty-six touchdowns by rushing—sixteen more than their nearest rival.

Unlike some years, when kicking was a problem for Green Bay, the 1962 Packers also had the best field goal percentage: 71.4 percent of those attempted.

Further reflecting the team's dominance, eleven men made the All-League squad of thirty players selected by Associated Press, United Press International, and Newspaper Enterprise Association. These included tight end Ron Kramer, tackle Forrest Gregg, guard Jerry Kramer, guard Fred Thurston, center Jim Ringo, and fullback Jim Taylor on the offensive team; end Willie Davis, tackle Henry Jordan, linebackers Dan Currie and Bill Forester, and corner back Herb Adderley on the defensive team.

The Giants won the Eastern Conference championship with nearly as good a record as Green Bay, losing only two of fourteen games. Thanks to Tittle's passing, New York had scored thirty-five of its forty-nine touchdowns in the regular season in the air, compared with Green Bay's fourteen of fifty-three touchdowns by passing. The playoff was expected to be a test of whether a good ground game could beat a good passing game, but it turned out to be more a battle of stubborn defenses.

The Packers scored first. Midway in the first quarter, when their drive was stalled on the New York twenty-six yard line, Jerry Kramer booted a field goal. That 3 to 0 margin stayed on the scoreboard until less than three minutes were left of the first half, when Taylor took a handoff seven yards from the New York goal line and ran for a touchdown. The Packers led 10-0 at the half.

Green Bay's punting was troublesome that December 30 in Yankee Stadium—its punts averaged only 25.5 yards, compared with 42 yards for New York—and halfway through the third quarter a blocked punt bounced back into the Packers' end zone. Jim Collier pounced on it for a touchdown, and when Don Chandler kicked the extra point for New York the score was 10 to 7.

A few minutes later, Jerry Kramer kicked a twenty-nine yard field goal, and with less than two minutes left in the fourth quarter he kicked another, giving Green Bay its 16 to 7 margin.

Tittle threw the ball forty-one times for eighteen completions and one interception, gaining a total of 197 yards. Starr, on the other hand, tried only twenty-one passes, completing nine. Green Bay gained 148 yards on the ground, compared with 94 for New York.

The Giants had a total of 291 yards gained, compared with 244 for Green Bay, and each team had eighteen first downs. But the Packers' defense held when Tittle's team pressed too close to the goal line, and it should be noted that New York's only score came from the blocked punt.

Gross receipts, including radio and television, amounted to $1,243,110. Each Packer got $5,888.57 for his afternoon's work. Each losing player's share was $4,166.85.

1963 Season

The opener was held at City Stadium in Green Bay, with Lombardi's team hoping for a third straight season as national champions. Before the afternoon was over, it was plain that 1963 would not see a repetition of 1962's nearly unbroken string of Packer successes.

Jerry Kramer kicked a forty-one-yard field goal in the first quarter, but the Chicago Bears also made a field goal in that period. The score was still 3 to 3 at the half. In the third quarter, Chicago went ahead with a touchdown.

The Packers' offense was having the kind of an afternoon a coach sees in his nightmares. The Bears intercepted four Green Bay passes— nearly half as many interceptions as opposing teams had managed during the entire 1962 season—and held the Packers to a total gain of merely 150 yards.

The Packers got no closer than thirty yards from the Bears' goal line, and for the first time in six games of the two cities' rivalry, Chicago won. The score: 10 to 3.

The season's second game was with Detroit, and at Milwaukee County Stadium the Packers seemed to have recovered their old skills. As Paul Hornung's replacement, Tom Moore gained 122 yards. Taylor added another 82. Green Bay had a 10 to 0 lead at halftime on a Kramer field goal and a Taylor touchdown. The Lions managed a 36-yard field goal in the third quarter, but Moore ran 15 yards for a touchdown to make it 17 to 3.

In the fourth quarter, Milt Plum threw a touchdown pass to bring Detroit within seven points of the Packers, but then Moore broke loose for a seventy-seven yard run for a touchdown and, a little later, Starr's pass to Max McGee was good for another. The score: Green Bay 31, Detroit 10.

Baltimore came to Green Bay for the season's third game. During the first half it seemed like a replay of the Bears game, with the Packers unable to score and the Colts taking a 7 to 0 lead. Boyd Dowler scored a touchdown on a Starr pass in the third quarter and Moore ran for another to put the Packers ahead 14 to 7. But the Colts converted a Packer fumble into a touchdown to tie the score, and late in the same quarter Baltimore added a field goal.

Trailing 17 to 14 in the fourth quarter, the Packers fumbled again. This time, however, Starr recovered the ball. Instead of falling on it, as is the custom, he dodged Baltimore tacklers and threw a pass to Boyd Dowler, converting a Green Bay error into a thirty-five-yard touchdown play.

Baltimore managed a fifty-two-yard field goal later in the period, but Starr's play had turned the game around. The Packers added a field goal of their own, along with another touchdown, and the final score was Green Bay 31, Baltimore 20.

Back at City Stadium in Green Bay for the season's fourth game, the Packers kept their momentum. Herb Adderley got things off to a fine start by running back a Los Angeles kick for ninety-eight yards and a touchdown. The Rams tied the game after intercepting a Zeke Bratkowski pass, but Green Bay went ahead again when Willie Davis tackled Roman Gabriel in the Los Angeles end zone for a safety.

The Packers led by only 15 to 10 at the half, but they scored 20 points in the third quarter and added another touchdown in the fourth, meanwhile holding Los Angeles scoreless. The score: Green Bay 42, Los Angeles 10.

In the season's fifth week, the Packers played Minnesota. They went about their chores in workmanlike fashion in the first half, taking a 24 to 7 lead. In the third quarter, Green Bay made it 27 to 7 with a field goal, but then the Vikings struck back.

A fumble recovery led to a third quarter touchdown for Minnesota. Kramer kicked another field goal, but in the fourth quarter Fran Tarkenton threw a touchdown pass and Minnesota scored another touchdown on the ground. With two minutes left, Green Bay's lead had been cut to 30 to 28 and Minnesota was only ten yards from the Packers' goal.

The defense held. The Vikings lined up for what seemed a certain field goal, but Herb Adderley blocked the kick and Hank Gremminger picked up the ball and ran eighty yards for a touchdown. The final score: Packers 37, Minnesota 28.

The sixth game was at St. Louis. The Packers scored the first five times they got the ball and led 20 to 0 at halftime. The Cardinals managed only one touchdown, with the Packers adding another 10 points in the second half. The game was costly, however. Before it was over, Bart Starr's hand was broken. The victory meant Green Bay was tied with Chicago for first place in the Western Conference. The final score: Green Bay 30, St. Louis 7.

At Baltimore in the seventh week of play, John Roach started at quarterback for Green Bay. The defense held the Colts to one field goal in the first half. Meanwhile, the Packers were taking advantage of Baltimore mistakes to lead 17 to 3 at the end of the second quarter.

Johnny Unitas finally started moving his team effectively in the fourth quarter and the score was tied 20 to 20 when Green Bay blocked a forty-seven-yard field goal attempt. Then Elijah Pitts scored one touchdown, Taylor another, and Roach had won his game as Starr's substitute. During the afternoon, Green Bay recovered four Colts fumbles and intercepted two passes. The final score: Green Bay 34, Baltimore 20.

At Milwaukee for the eighth game, Pittsburgh scored first to take a 7 to 0 lead. Roach was the Packers' quarterback and his team scored no touchdowns in the first half. Jerry Kramer kicked a field goal in the first quarter and added two more field goals in the second, so Green Bay had a 9 to 7 lead at the half.

In the third quarter, the Packers' ground game began to click. Jim Taylor scored a touchdown—he was to rush for 141 yards before the afternoon was over—and Pitts made another. Pitts scored again in the fourth quarter, matching Pittsburgh's second touchdown of the day, and Kramer kicked a 37-yard field goal, giving him the first four-field-goal day of his career. The final score: Green Bay 33, Pittsburgh 14.

In a rematch with Minnesota the Packers made their season's record 9-1. Roach was still quarterbacking and once again the first half was close, with each team scoring a touchdown. In the third quarter, Roach threw his second touchdown pass of the day to put Green Bay ahead, and in the fourth quarter another Roach pass gave the Packers a third touchdown. Bratkowski relieved Roach late in the game and threw a pass to Tom Moore, which resulted in the day's final score. The Packers won, 28 to 7.

The season's showdown came in the tenth game, played at Wrigley Field. Chicago, which had barely managed to whip Los Angeles the week before, had also lost only one game so the winner would take over first place in the Western Conference.

The Bears had allowed the Rams to gain only fifty-nine yards on the ground and twenty-nine yards in the air the previous week, and the Packers spent nearly as frustrating an afternoon trying to dent the Chicago defensive line. Meanwhile, four field goals kicked by Roger Leclerc plus two touchdowns gave the Bears a 26 to O lead. Moore's fourth-quarter touchdown on an eleven-yard running play kept Green Bay from being shut out, but the Packers had lost their first season series since 1959 and were pushed back into second place in the standings. The final score, Green Bay 7, Chicago 26.

During the eleventh week of play, Chicago was behind 17 to 14 with less than five minutes left to play in its game with Pittsburgh. But Leclerc kicked a field goal and the game ended in a 17-17 tie, keeping the Bears in first place.

Meanwhile, Bart Starr had returned for the first time since his injury in St. Louis. He hit Dowler with a touchdown pass in the first quarter, giving the Packers a 7 to 0 lead over San Francisco. In the second, Elijah Pitts surprised not only the Forty-Niners but 45,905 delighted fans in Milwaukee's County Stadium by throwing a touchdown pass to Ron Kramer.

After a San Francisco field goal, Taylor made a thirty-four-yard run for a touchdown and Pitts proved his versatility by scoring another, running with the ball this time. The Packers failed to score in the second half but it didn't matter. The score: Green Bay 28, San Francisco 10.

The season's twelfth game was played on Thanksgiving Day in Detroit. The teams were tied 6 to 6 at the end of the third quarter, then Starr hit Ron Kramer with a pass for a touchdown. In the final minutes, the Lions put together a seventy-eight-yard march, finally scoring from the one-yard line to tie the game, 13-13. The finish was disappointing for the Packers, who took small consolation in knowing that they would have the holiday off next year—the series that Green Bay and Detroit had been playing on Thanksgiving Day since 1951 was now ended. Beginning in 1964, other opponents for Detroit were to be rotated for the holiday games.

With the Packers still in second place and only two games to go, there was hope that San Francisco would be able to repeat its earlier victory over Chicago, making it possible for Green Bay to move back into a tie with the Bears for first place. But on the first play from scrimmage, Willie Galimore scored on a fifty-one-yard run and the Chicagoans went on to whip the Forty-Niners 27 to 7.

At Los Angeles, Green Bay scored first with McGee making a touchdown on a Starr pass. The Rams picked up two touchdowns in the second quarter, however, and led at the half, 14 to 10.

For the first time that season, the Packers had given up two touchdowns in the first half. In the second half, Green Bay got its revenge. McGee scored two more touchdowns on pass plays and Taylor ran forty yards for another. The final score: Green Bay 31, Los Angeles 14.

The season's final game was played on a Saturday in San Francisco in the interests of giving television fans a full weekend of football. To tie Chicago, it was necessary for Green Bay to win, then hope that Detroit could beat the Bears the next day.

Moore scored the first touchdown, giving Green Bay a 7 to 0 lead at the end of the first quarter. The Forty-Niners tied the game in the second quarter. The Packers went ahead again on a fifty-three-yard pass play, Starr to Dowler, but San Francisco matched this touchdown and the teams were tied 14 to 14 at the half.

Dowler caught another touchdown pass in the third quarter, putting the Packers ahead to stay. The best the Forty-Niners could do in the second half was a forty-four-yard field goal. The final score: Green Bay 21, San Francisco 17.

In the Detroit-Chicago game on Sunday, the Lions had a 7 to 3 lead at the half, but the Bears scored two touchdowns in the third quarter and went on to win the game and conference championship, 24 to 14. Chicago administered New York's third post-season loss in a row in the championship playoff, winning 14 to 10.

In the Playoff Bowl, a contest for also-rans, the Packers and the Browns played in Miami. Despite Lombardi's scorn for a game featuring second-place teams, the Packers won. Starr threw fifteen pass completions out of eighteen attempts before the coach put in Bratkowski and Roach. Green Bay led by 28 to 10 at the half and 35 to 10 at the three-quarter mark and was outscored only in the final quarter, when it no longer mattered very much. The final score: Green Bay 40, Cleveland 23.

Regular season record: 11 wins, 2 losses, 1 tie
Postseason record: 1-0

1964 Season

Jim Taylor's 1,169 yards gained on the ground was second only to Cleveland's Jim Brown, and Bart Starr recaptured his title as league champion quarterback from Y. A. Tittle by leading in percentage of completions (59.9 percent) and fewest interceptions (4 of 272 attempts for a remarkable 1.5 percent). Still, this season was one of Green Bay's less glorious under Vince Lombardi.

The previous year, it had lost only to the Bears. In the opening game Green Bay avoided the humiliation of three defeats in a row in the old rivalry. McGee scored on a pass play to give the Packers a first-quarter lead. In the second quarter, after a Chicago field goal, Moore took a Starr pass to make it 14-3. Hornung added three field goals before the afternoon was over. The final score: Green Bay 23, Chicago 12.

In the season's second game, the Colts took a 21 to 13 lead in the first half, then were held scoreless for the rest of the game. The halftime score would have been 21 to 14 if Hornung had not missed the point after the Packers' second touchdown, a failure that turned out to be decisive after Green Bay came within a single point of tying the game in the third quarter on Taylor's twenty-three-yard touchdown run. Two of Baltimore's three pass interceptions came at crucial moments in the second half. The final score was Baltimore 21, Green Bay 20.

Green Bay's third game of the season was played in Detroit on a Monday night—by now, television fans were having to stay home on Monday nights as well as weekends. Hornung scored one touchdown and Starr ran for another in the second quarter, giving the Packers a 14-3 lead at the half. Early in the third quarter, Bart's shoulder was injured. He left the game and Green Bay was held scoreless during the last half.

The defense managed to hold the Lions to a single fourth-quarter touch-down, however. The final score: Green Bay 14, Detroit 10.

The fourth week, Starr was back in action. Minnesota scored the first touchdown in the second quarter, but Bart hit Dowler for a fifty-yard pass play. The Vikings' middle linebacker, Rip Hawkins, blocked Hornung's attempted point after touchdown, and once again, as in the Baltimore game, the single point proved decisive.

With ninety seconds left in the game, Green Bay was ahead, 23 to 21, and Minnesota had the ball on its own twenty-yard line. But the Vikings got to the Packers' twenty-seven with eighteen seconds left to play and Fred Cox's field goal was good. The final score: Minnesota 24, Green Bay 23.

Moving into the fifth week of the season, the Packers had a 2-2 record, though both their losses had been by a single point. San Francisco was next and the game at Milwaukee County Stadium drew a record 47,547 fans.

Each team scored a touchdown in the first half, then Hornung put the Packers ahead with a third-quarter field goal. San Francisco went ahead 14 to 10 on its second touchdown, but Taylor was having a good day—he gained 133 yards on the ground before the afternoon was over—and early in the fourth quarter he broke through the middle of the Forty-Niners' line for a 27-yard touchdown run. Dowler caught a Starr pass late in the game for another touchdown. The final score: Green Bay 24, San Francisco 14.

The sixth week featured a rematch with the Colts, who had lost their opener to Minnesota, then won four straight. Green Bay had a 14 to 7 lead at the half, but Baltimore score 10 points in the third quarter to go ahead 17 to 14. In the fourth quarter, Pitts grabbed a punt and ran sixty-five yards for a touchdown that gave the Packers a four-point margin. Once again, an attempted kick proved Green Bay's undoing. With two minutes left to play, a field goal attempt was blocked. Jerry Logan ran the ball to the Packers' thirty. Two plays later, it was on Green Bay's five. From there, Lenny Moore carried it over for a touchdown that put Green Bay's season record back at the .500 mark. The final score: Baltimore 24, Green Bay 21.

The seventh game was with the Rams and for much of the first two periods it seemed that the Packers would run away with it. They led 17 to 0 on a Taylor touchdown, a Hornung field goal, and a forty-two-yard touchdown run by Willie Wood after a pass interception. Then Los Angeles struck for two quick touchdowns, one by air and one on the ground, so the half ended with the Packers' lead cut to 17-14.

In the third period, the Rams blocked a Packer field goal attempt and Bobby Smith ran the ball ninety-four yards for a touchdown. Los Angeles added two field goals later in the game. The final score: Los Angeles 27, Green Bay 17.

With the season record now at 3-4, the Packers started the scoring in the rematch with Minnesota when McGee caught a Starr pass for a touchdown. The Vikings also scored in the first quarter, making it 7 to 7, but in the second period Taylor caught Starr's passes for two touchdowns and Moore scored another on a twenty-six-yard run. Bart's fourth touchdown pass of the day went to Max McGee in the fourth quarter and Taylor added a final score on a one-yard run. The results: Green Bay 42, Minnesota 13.

Back at the .500 mark, the Packers entertained the visiting Lions by demonstrating that all those touchdown passes of the week before did not mean Lombardi had abandoned his ground game. Green Bay gained 232 yards on the ground, including an 84-yard touchdown by Jim Taylor in the first quarter, the longest gain from scrimmage in the NFL in four years. The Packers scored 30 points before Detroit got on the scoreboard late in the fourth quarter. The final score: Green Bay 30, Detroit 7.

In the season's tenth week, San Francisco experimented with a rookie quarterback, George Mira, who completed ten of seventeen passes. Green Bay led, 14 to 10, at the half, but the Forty-Niners held the visiting team scoreless for the rest of the game. The final score: San Francisco 24, Green Bay 14.

Once more back at the .500 mark, the Packers played Cleveland in Milwaukee, gave up two touchdowns in the first quarter, and trailed by 14 to 7 at the half. But in the third period, Taylor and Starr each scored a touchdown on short runs, with Taylor going over for another in the fourth quarter. The final score: Green Bay 28, Cleveland 21.

The season's twelfth game was played at the Cotton Bowl, with Green Bay moving out to a 17-14 halftime lead after Henry Jordan made a sixty-yard touchdown run after recovering a Dallas fumble. Lionel Aldridge struck another blow for the linemen later in the game, scoring on another Cowboys fumble. Green Bay scored twenty-eight points in the second half and won the game, 45-21.

The Chicago-Green Bay rivalry moved to Wrigley Field for the season's thirteenth game. Hornung and Taylor each scored a touchdown, Willie Wood's long punt returns putting the Packers in position for the scores. Wood intercepted a Bears pass and Herb Adderley grabbed two. The final score: Green Bay 17, Chicago 3.

With the last game of the season ahead, Baltimore had clinched the Western Conference championship, but Green Bay could come in second if it tied or won from the Rams. Los Angeles scored two touchdowns in the first quarter and led 21 to 7 at the half. Green Bay trailed 21 to 10 after three quarters, and the Rams made it 24 to 10 with a fourth-quarter field goal. Then Boyd Dowler caught a Starr pass for a touchdown and Taylor, who gained 165 yards rushing that afternoon, went over for another to tie the game. The final score: Green Bay 24, Los Angeles 24.

In the championship game, Baltimore lost to Cleveland 27 to 0. As the Western Conference's representatives in the Playoff Bowl, the Packers did a little better, but they lost, too. They were behind 17 to 3 before Taylor scored two last-quarter touchdowns to make the final score respectable: St. Louis 24, Green Bay 17.

Regular season record: 8 wins, 5 losses, 1 tie
Postseason record: 0-1

1965 Season

The season that was the start of Green Bay's three-year championship streak did not begin auspiciously. At the opener in Pittsburgh, the Packers scored only one touchdown in the first half—it came on an Adderley interception—while permitting the Steelers to make three field goals for a 9 to 7 halftime lead.

The second half was another sort of game. Pittsburgh's scoring was over for the day, but Green Bay moved ahead on a Marv Fleming touchdown and two Don Chandler field goals in the third quarter, then scored three additional touchdowns in the final period, two of them by Pitts. The final score: Green Bay 41, Pittsburgh 9.

Baltimore was the team Green Bay had to beat that year and at Milwaukee County Stadium the Packers rose to the challenge. With the score tied 3 to 3 in the second quarter, Adderley intercepted a Unitas pass and ran forty-four yards for a touchdown. The Colts tied the score before the half ended, however, and the 10 to 10 tie continued through the third quarter. Chandler kicked a field goal in the fourth period to put the Packers ahead, but Unitas passed his team to another touchdown and a 17 to 13 lead.

Taylor had been unable to start and Starr was on the bench in the second half because of an injury, but Adderley was still in the game. He stopped a Baltimore drive deep in Green Bay territory by recovering a fumble late in the game. Zeke Bratkowski hit McGee for a thirty-seven-yard touchdown that kept the Packers undefeated. The final score: Green Bay 20, Baltimore 17.

For the season's third game, the Bears visited Lambeau Field, now enlarged to accommodate 50,852 spectators that day. Green Bay dominated the first half, leading 20 to 0 at intermission, but Gale Sayers scored two touchdowns in the second. Chicago gained 413 yards to 299 for Green Bay, with Starr's passes responsible for all but 36 of those yards, but the final score was Green Bay 23, Chicago 14.

The following Sunday's game was with San Francisco. Don Chandler put the Packers in position for their only first-quarter touchdown when he made a twenty-seven-yard run from punt formation. Later, he booted a ninety-yard punt, the second longest in league history. The Packers scored touchdowns in the first, third, and fourth quarters to go with Chandler's two field goals in the second period. The final score: Green Bay 27, San Francisco 10.

In the season's fifth game, with the Packers still unbeaten, Detroit took a 21 to 3 lead in the first half. But in the third quarter, Starr completed seven of eight passes, good for 225 yards and three touchdowns. In the fourth quarter, the quarterback crossed the goal line on a four-yard running play. Meanwhile, the Packer defense had held the Lions scoreless during the last half. The final score: Green Bay 31, Detroit 21.

Green Bay and Dallas met in Milwaukee for the next game. The defensive teams dominated the first half, which ended with the Packers ahead 3 to 0. In the third quarter, the Cowboys fumbled twice and Green Bay turned both mistakes into scores—a Chandler field goal and a Taylor touchdown. The pass defenses were notable—Dallas lost one more yard than it gained through the air and Green Bay had a minus-ten passing average. The final score: Green Bay 13, Dallas 3.

Still unbeaten after six games, the Packers had an unfriendly reception from the Bears at Wrigley Field. Taylor put Green Bay ahead with a first-quarter touchdown and Chandler added a second-quarter field goal, but Chicago scored 17 points in the second period and added touchdowns in each of the last two quarters. The final score: Chicago 31, Green Bay 10.

The rematch with Detroit, held at Lambeau Field, was one of Starr's most frustrating afternoons. He was thrown eleven times for losses adding up to 109 yards. In the fourth quarter, he was tackled in the end zone for a safety. An interception of one of his passes led to the Lions' only touchdown. The final score: Detroit 12, Green Bay 7.

After seeming unbeatable in the first six games, the Packers now had a two-game losing streak and showed a remarkable inability to score for most of the Rams game at Milwaukee. Los Angeles also spent most of the afternoon huffing and puffing without moving very far. Both teams scored field goals in the first quarter, but the second and third periods were scoreless. With about a minute left in the game, Green Bay finally took advantage of a break. Lionel Aldridge recovered a fumble and Don Chandler hit a seven-yard field goal. The final score: Green Bay 6, Los Angeles 3.

Following the first NFL game in two years in which neither team scored a touchdown, the Packers played Minnesota in what turned out to be a high-scoring game. Only one touchdown was scored in the first half—Carroll Dale caught the first touchdown pass Starr had thrown in three weeks. Minnesota went ahead 13 to 10 in the third quarter, but in the final period the Packers finally began to put their offensive talents to use. Dowler caught a Starr pass for a touchdown, Pitts ran for another, Doug Hart returned a fumble for a third, then Long caught another pass for the fourth touchdown in the quarter, which tied an NFL record. The final score: Green Bay 38, Minnesota 13.

For the season's eleventh game, Green Bay went to Los Angeles where the Rams were suffering from an eight-game losing streak. Green Bay led briefly in the first quarter on a Chandler field goal. Then Roman Gabriel put an attack together and the Rams' defense made life difficult for the visitors from the Midwest. By the time the Packers scored their only touchdown, it was late in the fourth quarter and Los Angeles was in full command. The final score: Los Angeles 21, Green Bay 10.

Trailing the Colts by one and a half games in the Western Conference standings, the Packers could only hope Baltimore would stumble. Meanwhile, there was a game to be played with Minnesota, which tied the score in the first quarter after Starr had hit Dowler with a touchdown pass. Pitts scored in the second quarter, but the Vikings managed to make three field goals and led at the half, 16 to 14.

Bratkowski replaced Starr in the third quarter and put together a touchdown drive that sent the Packers ahead to stay. The final score: Green Bay 24, Minnesota 19.

Meanwhile, the Packers' old enemies, the mighty Bears line, was being helpful. Chicago held Baltimore scoreless and put Johnny Unitas out for the season with a knee injury. Sayers, who was having quite a rookie season, made the game's only touchdown. Chicago won, 13 to 0, to put the Packers only a half game out of first.

As luck would have it, the Colts were next on the schedule. The word used for the game was "crucial." Baltimore took the lead with a first-quarter field goal, but then Hornung scored a touchdown on a two-yard run and caught a pass for another. With Gary Cuozzo pitching passes in place of Unitas, the Colts fought back with a touchdown and field goal in the second quarter, but Starr hit Dowler for another score and Green Bay led at the half, 21 to 13.

In the third quarter, Hornung scored two touchdowns on power plays, and in the final period he made his fifth of the day on a pass play that went sixty-five yards. This was more than enough to win, even though Baltimore managed to score fourteen points in the last quarter. The final score: Green Bay 42, Baltimore 27.

With one game to go, the Packers were in first place. To win the Western Conference title, they needed a victory over San Francisco, which had a 7-6 record and had been whipped the week before by Chicago, 61 to 20. Meanwhile, the Colts were going into their final game with the Rams without a regular quarterback, Cuozzo having joined Unitas on the sidelines as the result of an injury. Tom Matte was assigned to the job, but he was supposed to be a halfback.

The Baltimore-Los Angeles game was played on Saturday, giving the Packers a chance to watch it on television. If the Rams won, the conference competition was over. But they lost, 20 to 17, which meant Green Bay had to beat the Forty-Niners to become champs.

Midway in the fourth quarter, the Packers were behind, 17 to 14. Then Starr put together a drive that reached the San Francisco five and Taylor took the ball from there to score a touchdown. A little later, Chandler kicked a thirty-one-yard field goal to give Green Bay a 24 to 17 lead. The Forty-Niners fought back and with with a little more than a minute to play, John Brodie threw a touchdown pass that tied the game. The final score: Green Bay 24, San Francisco 24.

Now that the Packers and Colts had identical records of 10-3-1, a playoff was necessary to decide the conference championship. It was held December 26 in Green Bay, with Matte quarterbacking for Baltimore and Bratkowski replacing Starr when he was injured on the first play from scrimmage.

The Colts won the first half 10 to 0, scoring a touchdown on a fumble recovery and kicking a field goal. Hornung scored from the one-yard line in the third quarter to make it 10-7, and in the fourth period Chandler's controversial field goal from the twenty-two tied the score. In an overtime period in which the first team to score would win, Baltimore missed a field goal, then Chandler hit one from the twenty-five-yard line. The final score: Green Bay 13, Baltimore 10.

Cleveland had won the Eastern Conference with an 11-3 record that required no such last minute heroics. The league championship game was held January 2, 1966, in Green Bay. It was fairly even in the first half, with the Browns winning the first quarter, 9 to 7, and the Packers scoring two field goals in the second period to Cleveland's one. That made it 13 to 12 at the half with Green Bay leading.

The second half saw the Packers' defense tighten to keep the eastern champions from scoring a single point. Hornung went over from the thirteen-yard line for a third-quarter touchdown, and Chandler kicked a fourth-quarter field goal. The final score: Green Bay 23, Cleveland 12.

Regular season record: 10 wins, 3 losses, 1 tie
Postseason record: 2-0

1966 Season

Between the playoff game with Baltimore in 1965 and the opening game of the 1966 season, the Packers had been listening to claims that the Colts had lost through a questionable decision on Chandler's fourth-quarter field goal. Now they had a chance to prove they could beat the East Coast rivals, even though Unitas was healthy again.

Neither team could score in the first quarter. Baltimore got the first points in the second with a field goal. But then linebacker Lee Roy Caffey ran back a pass interception fifty-two yards for a touchdown and, a little later in the same quarter, Bob Jeter grabbed another Unitas pass out of the air and dodged his way for forty-six yards to the goal line. That made the score 14 to 3 and the game was as good as over. According to the league rules, the second half had to be played, however, and the Packers added another ten points on Starr's run for a touchdown and a Chandler field goal. The final score: Green Bay 24, Baltimore 3.

Another rematch of postseason rivals was scheduled for the second week, with Green Bay traveling to Cleveland and a game before 83,943 persons, the third largest crowd in that city's history. They got their money's worth. The Browns, who had not distinguished themselves in the championship game the previous January, pulled out to a 14 to 0 lead before Hornung took a Starr pass and made it 14 to 7.

It was 17 to 7 at the half, but in the third quarter Taylor shoved over from the one to bring the Packers within three points of Cleveland. Lou Groza, the Browns' veteran kicker, made the margin six points by hitting a forty-six-yard field goal in the fourth quarter, but Starr moved his team down the field and with less than three minutes to play hit Taylor with a short pass that put the Packers ahead. The final score: Green Bay 21, Cleveland 20.

The third game of the season was with Los Angeles, which had won its first two games. But Hornung had scored two touchdowns and Chandler had kicked a field goal before the Rams got on the scoreboard, and the Packers spent an enjoyable afternoon jumping on quarterback Roman Gabriel, who was thrown eight times. Starr was having a more successful afternoon, passing for two touchdowns and 257 yards, including an 80-yard pass play in the final quarter. The final score: Green Bay 24, Los Angeles 13.

On the season's fourth Sunday, quarterback Milt Plum completed fifteen of twenty-four passes for Detroit. But two others were intercepted by Green Bay defenders, who also pounced on three Lions fumbles during an afternoon when Detroit outgained Green Bay, 349 yards to 251, but couldn't outscore them. Despite all those yards, the Lions were held to two touchdowns. The final score: Green Bay 23, Detroit 14.

The Packers took their 4-0 record to Kezar Stadium where John Brodie's replacement, George Mira, gave them an unpleasant afternoon. He threw two touchdown passes and made a thirty-eight-yard run that led to another. Starr countered with two touchdown passes of his own and Chandler kicked two field goals. The final score: San Francisco 21, Green Bay 20.

Having lost to a team that had been unable to win any of its previous games, the Packers headed for Chicago with plans to stop the unstoppable Gale Sayers. They did, almost. He ran for only twenty-nine yards and the Bears were shut out. The final score: Green Bay 17, Chicago 0.

In the season's seventh week, the Packers had a relaxing afternoon for a change. Atlanta, an expansion team, never had a chance. Green Bay had twenty-eight points on the scoreboard before the Falcons kicked a field goal for their only points of the day. Donny Anderson, the Packers' high-priced rookie, had a chance for his first extended experience in a professional game and scored two touchdowns, one from five yards out, the other on a seventy-seven-yard punt return. Herb Adderley tied a league record by scoring the fifth touchdown of his career on an interception. Doug Hart also scored on an intercepted pass. The final score: Green Bay 56, Atlanta 3.

Leading the Western Conference by a game and a half, the Packers played Detroit in another one-sided game. Elijah Pitts came within three feet of gaining 100 yards on the ground, the best day of his career, and scored three touchdowns. The final score: Green Bay 31, Detroit 7.

In the Minnesota game, the Packers won the first three quarters, leading 17 to 10 when the final period began. Then Fran Tarkenton's scrambling became effective, and the Vikings rallied for a touchdown and a field goal. The final score: Minnesota 20, Green Bay 17.

Green Bay had the season's tenth Sunday off—league expansion had complicated the schedule—but it was not a particularly pleasant holiday. Baltimore defeated Atlanta to gain a half game on the idle Packers and move into a first-place tie in the Western Conference.

The Bears were next. In the first quarter, after Starr was injured on a pass play, Bratkowski came in and threw a touchdown pass to Carroll Dale, which put the Packers ahead 7 to 0. The score stayed the same until the fourth quarter, when Sayers ran for a touchdown. The point after touchdown was not made, but Bratkowski was not happy with the 7 to 6 margin and threw Dale another touchdown pass to give Green Bay a little breathing room. The Packers also failed to make the point after touchdown, but it didn't matter much. The Colts, meanwhile, had lost to Detroit 20 to 14 and Green Bay was alone in first place again. The final score: Green Bay 13, Chicago 6.

The twelfth week featured a rematch between Tarkenton's Vikings and the Packers. Starr, who had been hampered by a leg injury, was back in action and threw for two touchdowns. Jim Grabowski, the other half of the Packers' million dollar rookie combination, scored his first touchdown on a thirty-six-yard run. Minnesota had to be content with field goals until the final quarter, when a Tarkenton pass finally resulted in a touchdown. The final score: Green Bay 28, Minnesota 16.

With a two-game lead and three games to go, Green Bay needed to win over San Francisco to cinch a tie for the second straight conference championship. The game was played in Milwaukee under frigid conditions, but Starr ignored the icy field and completed thirteen passes for 236 yards and one touchdown, an 83-yard play in the first quarter. The score stayed 7 to 0 until the final period, when Starr ran for a touchdown from the one-yard line. The Forty-Niners countered with a touchdown pass from John Brodie, but Pitts matched that with a score from the two. The final score: Green Bay 20, San Francisco 7.

By winning all its remaining games, Baltimore could still tie if Green Bay lost theirs. The two teams met in Memorial Stadium in the Colts' home city. Once again, Bratkowski came off the bench when Starr was injured and was equal to the occasion. Baltimore led 10 to 7 at the half, but in the final quarter Pitts scored, then Willie Davis spoiled Unitas' plans to recapture the lead with a jarring tackle that caused the Colts' quarterback to fumble on the Green Bay nine-yard line with a minute to play. The Packers had won their second conference title in a row and their fifth in seven years under Lombardi. The final score: Green Bay 14, Baltimore 10.

Having defeated Baltimore for the fifth time in two seasons, the Packers played the season's last game against the Rams, with Bratkowski handling the quarterbacking. After Los Angeles had scored first with a field goal in the early minutes of the game, Bob Jeter intercepted a Roman Gabriel pass on the Packers' twenty-five and ran it back for a touchdown, giving Green Bay six such scores during the year to tie a league record.

Bruce Gossett kicked three field goals for the Rams that afternoon, giving him twenty-eight for the season. After trailing most of the afternoon Los Angeles pulled to within four points by scoring two late touchdowns. The final score: Green Bay 27, Los Angeles 23.

In the NFL championship game, played at the Cotton Bowl, Green Bay pulled out to a fourteen-point lead with touchdowns by Pitts and Grabowski before Dallas had scored a point. Before the first quarter was over, however, the Cowboys tied the score on Don Meredith's passing and the running of Dan Reeves and Don Perkins.

The Dallas defense held the Packers to 102 yards and only three first downs rushing. Starr was also having his problems with the defense, which got to him five times during the game when he was trying to pass. But when he got the ball away it was usually caught by a Packer, giving him nineteen completions out of twenty-eight attempts.

Carroll Dale scored on a fifty-one-yard pass play in the second quarter and Green Bay led 21 to 17 at the half. After the intermission, Dallas pulled ahead on a pair of field goals, but Starr's passes to Dowler and McGee were good for a pair of touchdowns before Meredith threw a fourth-quarter touchdown pass. The final score: Green Bay 34, Dallas 27.

The gross receipts had climbed to $2,773,861.20, which gave each Packer $9,813.63 to spend.

The first AFL-NFL championship game was played in the Los Angeles Coliseum January 15, 1967, with the Packers meeting Kansas City in what was christened the Super Bowl.

Len Dawson, the AFL team's quarterback, came close to matching Starr in the statistics, completing sixteen of twenty-seven passes compared with sixteen of twenty-three for Starr. The Packers scored first on a thirty-seven-yard pass play to McGee, but in the second quarter Dawson hit Curtis McClinton, his fullback, with a seven-yarder to tie the score. Jim Taylor ran for another Packer touchdown, then Kansas City managed a field goal before the half to bring the score to 14-10.

The second half was a different sort of game. The Packers defense held the AFL champs scoreless while Green Bay made three touchdowns, two of them by Pitts. The final score: Green Bay 35, Kansas City 10.

Regular season record: 12 wins, 2 losses
Postseason record: 2-0

1967 Season

For the first time, the NFL was divided into four divisions—the Central and Coastal in the Western Conference, the Capitol and Century divisions in the Eastern. Green Bay was in the Central Division, along with Chicago, Detroit, and Minnesota.

In seeking their third straight world championship, the Packers got off to a discouraging start. The opener was with Detroit, which scored a touchdown in the first quarter on an intercepted pass—one of four of

Starr's passes to be caught by Lions players during the afternoon. Detroit added a field goal and another touchdown to lead Green Bay 17 to 0 at the half.

Pitts scored a touchdown in the third quarter and another in the fourth, but the Packers were still three points behind with less than two minutes left when they got a final chance to score. The offense pushed the ball to Detroit's twenty-eight-yard line but was stopped there. Don Chandler's field goal tied the score. The results: Green Bay 17, Detroit 17.

In the season's second game, the Packers pulled out to a 10-0 lead in the first half on a touchdown by Jim Grabowski and a Chandler field goal. But Chicago caught up in the fourth quarter while the Green Bay offense reached new heights of frustration. Starr threw three interceptions and Grabowski, who was having his first 100-yard rushing game, fumbled the ball away three times. Once again, Chandler came in to try a field goal with slightly over a minute to play. This one was from 46 yards out but he made it. The final score: Green Bay 13, Chicago 10.

Atlanta, the third opponent, was no match for the Packers even though Starr went out with an injury in the first quarter. Bratkowski passes to Carroll Dale were good for two touchdowns in the first half, and Willie Davis added two points by tackling an Atlanta ball carrier in the end zone. Ben Wilson ran for a fourth-quarter touchdown. The final score: Green Bay 23, Atlanta 0.

The fourth week, Detroit followed the script of the earlier Packers-Lions game by pulling out to an early lead. After a Detroit field goal, Larry Hand intercepted Bratkowski's pass and ran for a touchdown. A nineteen-yard pass play from Zeke to Donny Anderson made the margin 10-7 at the half. Chandler kicked a field goal to tie the game in the third quarter. Then Ray Nitschke grabbed a Detroit pass and scored, and Boyd Dowler caught a touchdown pass to put Green Bay safely ahead, despite another Lions touchdown late in the game. The final score: Green Bay 27, Detroit 17.

Intercepted passes were also important in the season's fifth game, played at Milwaukee. Dale and Bratkowski collaborated on an eighty-six-yard pass play that put the Packers ahead in the second quarter, with neither team able to score in the third period. In the fourth, however, interceptions by Ed Sharockman and Earsell Mackbee led to a Minnesota touchdown and a Fred Cox field goal. The final score: Minnesota 10, Green Bay 6.

Starr was back in action the sixth week. Pitts scored a touchdown in the first quarter, but the Giants picked up two in the second, with Fran Tarkenton throwing the ball with his usual abandon. A Chandler field goal made the halftime score 14 to 10 in New York's favor.

The second half was more pleasant for Packer fans. Starr directed a Green Bay attack that scored thirty-eight points in the last two quarters. Grabowski had a good day, gaining 123 yards on the ground and catching a touchdown pass. The final score: Green Bay 48, New York 21.

The seventh week was lucky for Green Bay's Road Runner, Travis Williams, who made his first NFL touchdown on a 93-yard kickoff return. Before the season ended he was to set an NFL record by making four touchdowns on returned kickoffs and establish another record by averaging 41.1 yards on kickoff returns. Gale Sayers of Chicago also surpassed the old record that year with a 37.7-yard average.

Herb Adderley set a record, too. In the first quarter of the St. Louis game he intercepted one of Jim Hart's passes and ran for a touchdown, the sixth of his career. Hart threw for 317 yards and two touchdowns and Green Bay also scored freely. Green Bay was behind 23 to 17 when Williams made his lengthy kickoff return. Later in the fourth quarter, Starr's pass to Dowler added another score. The results: Green Bay 31, St. Louis 23.

When the Packers traveled to Baltimore for the season's eighth game, the Colts were unbeaten in the 1967 season. On the other hand, Baltimore hadn't been able to win from Green Bay in five previous attempts. The Packers led at the half, 3 to 0, and the third quarter was scoreless, which indicates the nature of the two teams' defensive games. In the fourth quarter, Starr hit Donny Anderson with a pass for the game's first touchdown, putting Green Bay ahead 10 to 0. Late in the game, Johnny Unitas passed for a touchdown but the kick was no good, leaving a four-point deficit. The Colts tried an on-side kick, a maneuver ordinarily attempted only in desperation. This time it worked. After Baltimore had recovered the ball, Unitas threw his second touchdown pass in less than a minute of play. The final score: Baltimore 13, Green Bay 10.

The Packers faced the Cleveland game without Pitts or Grabowski, who had been injured in Baltimore. They still had the Road Runner, however, and he was enough. He made two touchdowns on kickoff returns in the first quarter—one of 85 yards, the other of 87. In all, forty-two points were scored that quarter, thirty-five of them by the Packers. The

Browns were through scoring for the day, but Green Bay added another twenty points as the afternoon wore on, its offensive yardage adding up to an astonishing 456 yards. Donny Anderson started a game for the first time and scored four touchdowns. The results: Green Bay 55, Cleveland 7.

In the tenth week of play, Starr was injured in the second quarter of the game with San Francisco, but two field goals and an Anderson touchdown were enough to give the Packers the game when the defensive team held the Forty-Niners scoreless. This was Zeke Bratkowski's ninth win in ten games in which he'd relieved Starr. The score: Green Bay 13, San Francisco 0.

The Chicago game was next and Starr was back in action. So was Travis Williams, who nearly scored another touchdown on a kickoff return. He was stopped on the Bears' twenty-five after a sixty-nine-yard run. A few plays later, Donny Anderson scored to put Green Bay ahead, 14 to 7. At the half the score was 14 to 10, and each team scored a field goal in the second half. The Packers had cinched a first place finish in their division. The final score: Green Bay 17, Chicago 13.

The twelfth game was with Minnesota. Although the Vikings' Dave Osborn was having the best day of his career with a total gain on the ground of 155 yards, the Packers led during most of the game. But a touchdown pass from Joe Kapp and a field goal enabled Minnesota to tie the score at 27 to 27. With the game nearly over, Kapp fumbled on the Minnesota 28. Chandler's field goal from the 19 a few plays later put the Packers ahead with eight seconds remaining. The final score: Green Bay 30, Minnesota 27.

Los Angeles was fighting with Baltimore for the championship of the Coastal Division, and the Rams' game with Green Bay marked the first time that Memorial Coliseum in Los Angeles had sold out in advance, with 76,637 fans on hand. Green Bay scored first on a Starr pass to Dale, but the Rams made a touchdown to tie the game in the second quarter. Chandler's 32-yard field goal put the Packers ahead at the half. Roman Gabriel's second touchdown pass of the day and a field goal put Los Angeles seven points ahead in the third quarter, but then Travis Williams caught a kickoff four yards inside his own end zone and ran 104 yards for a touchdown.

A Rams field goal put the Packers behind again, but Chuck Mercein bulled his way from the four-yard line for a fourth-quarter touchdown that gave Green Bay the lead. Late in the game, Tony Guillory blocked

Donny Anderson's punt, a play that led to Gabriel's third touchdown pass with about half a minute remaining. The final score: Los Angeles 27, Green Bay 24.

The season's final game was with Pittsburgh, which hadn't won from the Packers since 1954. The Steelers scored a touchdown on an interception early in the game and, after a Chandler field goal, scored another to lead 14 to 3. The Packers made the halftime score 14-10 when Williams caught a pass from Don Horn, who was quarterbacking. Williams scored another touchdown on a twenty-five-yard run late in the game, but by that time the Steelers had added another ten points. The final score: Pittsburgh 24, Green Bay 17.

The Packers went into the Western Conference playoff with a two-game losing streak. The Rams, which had outscored them two weeks before, had been beaten only once during the season for a record of 11-1-2.

Gabriel threw a touchdown pass in the first quarter to give Los Angeles a 7 to 0 lead. Despite the bitterly cold afternoon in Milwaukee, Starr was having a fine day. Before the afternoon was over, he had completed seventeen of twenty-three passes, good for 222 yards. The rookie, Williams, broke loose in the second quarter for a 46-yard touchdown run that tied the score. Later in that period, Starr hit Dale for another touchdown. The Packers added a third quarter touchdown by Mercein and one in the fourth quarter by Williams. Meanwhile, the Green Bay defense had clamped down tight, stopping further scoring by the Rams. The final score: Green Bay 28, Los Angeles 7.

Meanwhile, Dallas had beaten Cleveland decisively—the score was 52 to 14. The divisional champions met at Green Bay to decide whether the Packers could win a third straight NFL title and go to their second Super Bowl playoff with the AFL titleholder.

Green Bay scored in the first quarter on a Starr pass to Dowler. The Packers led 14 to 0 in the second period when Dowler scored again on a forty-three-yard pass play. Then a Packer fumble led the way to a Cowboys touchdown and Danny Villanueva added three points with a field goal to make the halftime score 14 to 10.

Neither team could score in the third quarter, with the Packers hanging onto their slim lead in the subzero temperatures. In the fourth quarter, Green Bay's defenders were outfoxed when Dan Reeves took Don

Meredith's handoff, then passed to Lance Rentzel. The play was good for fifty yards and a touchdown that put Dallas ahead, 17 to 14.

The game's final score was the most dramatic touchdown in Lombardi's career at Green Bay. When Starr scored from the Dallas one-yard line, Green Bay had won its third league championship in a row. The final score: Green Bay 21, Dallas 17.

The Super Bowl game with the Oakland Raiders in Miami on January 14, 1968, was Lombardi's last game as the Packers' head coach. It began with two Chandler field goals and a sixty-two-yard pass play, Starr to Dowler, putting Green Bay ahead 13 to 0 before Daryle Lamonica threw a touchdown pass to Bill Miller to make it 13-7. Chandler added a forty-three-yard field goal before the first half ended.

The Packers scored ten points in the third quarter on a run by Donny Anderson and another field goal. Herb Adderley added another touchdown in the final period, running back an intercepted pass for sixty yards. Late in the game, Oakland scored its second touchdown on another Lamonica to Miller pass. The final score: Green Bay 33, Oakland 14.

Regular season record: 9 wins, 4 losses, 1 tie
Postseason record: 3-0

During Vince Lombardi's nine years as Green Bay's head coach, his team won its division championship six times, the league title five times, and the only two Super Bowl games it played.

The overall statistics:
Regular season record: 1959-1967: 89 wins, 29 losses, 4 ties
Postseason record: 10 wins, 2 losses

In all, the Packers won 99 games, lost 29, and tied 4, not counting 42 victories in exhibition games.

The Packers placed third in the Western Conference in 1959, behind Baltimore and Chicago; first in 1960, 1961, and 1962; second in 1963, a half game behind the Bears; second to Baltimore in 1964; first in 1965, 1966, and 1967.

1969 Season

With Lombardi as the Washington Redskins' head coach and vice-president, the team sought its first winning season since 1955.

The games went like this:

Washington 26, New Orleans 20
Cleveland 27, Washington 23
Washington 17, San Francisco 17
Washington 33, St. Louis 17
Washington 20, New York 14
Washington 14, Pittsburgh 7
Baltimore 41, Washington 17
Washington 28, Philadelphia 28
Dallas 41, Washington 28
Washington 27, Atlanta 20
Los Angeles 24, Washington 13
Washington 34, Philadelphia 29
Washington 17, New Orleans 14
Dallas 20, Washington 10.

In retrospect, the second New Orleans game was the crucial one. If the Redskins had lost, their season's record would have been 6-6-2. To rise above the .500 mark, a victory was essential.

Although the Saints' record was hardly distinguished—New Orleans wound up with a record of five wins and nine defeats—the Redskins' opponents gained 174 yards rushing that afternoon, compared with 91 for Washington. Even in the passing department, New Orleans covered more ground, gaining 162 yards through the air to 157 yards for Sonny Jurgensen.

Lombardi's team made fewer mistakes, however. It was penalized only ten yards, compared with seventy-three for the Saints. New Orleans lost the ball twice on interceptions and once on a fumble, while Washington had none of either.

The scoring began with Charley Harraway taking a handoff on the New Orleans twelve, finding a hole and running for a touchdown. Curt Knight made it 10 to 0 with a nineteen-yard field goal. Later in the first half, Harraway caught Jurgensen's pass for a thirty-yard touchdown play that put Washington ahead 17 to 0.

In the second half, Bill Kilmer was replaced by Edd Hargett as the Saints' quarterback, and the New Orleans attack began to be more effective. Mixing passes with a stubborn ground game, the Saints pushed down to the Washington one-yard line, from where Don Shy went in for a touchdown.

Later in the game, a five-yard run by Ernie Wheelright and the point after touchdown made the score 14 to 17 in Washington's favor. The Saints gained 336 yards during the game, nearly 100 yards more than Washington, but in the closing minutes the Redskins' defense held and a winning season was assured. The final score: Washington 17, New Orleans 14.

Lombardi's season with the Redskins coincided with Jurgensen's thirteenth as a professional quarterback. At the end of play in 1969, he had passed for a total of 26,978 yards during his career, putting him behind only Johnny Unitas and Y. A. Tittle among all the quarterbacks who had played in the league. He had scored 213 touchdowns on his passes, second only to Johnny Unitas' career total of 266.

During 1969, Jurgensen completed 276 of 442 passes for 3,102 yards and 22 touchdowns. Larry Brown led the team's rushers with 888 yards, the most ever gained by a Redskins rookie. Charley Taylor was the team's leading pass receiver, catching 71 for 883 yards, second in the league.

Lombardi's record during his one year in Washington was seven games won, five lost, two tied. That made his overall total for ten seasons as a pro head coach a remarkable 106 wins, 34 losses, and 6 ties.